Elizabeth Ettorre
Editor

Making Lesbians Visible in the Substance Use Field

Making Lesbians Visible in the Substance Use Field has been co-published simultaneously as *Journal of Lesbian Studies*, Volume 9, Number 3 2005.

Pre-publication REVIEWS, COMMENTARIES, EVALUATIONS...

"HELPS CLOSE AN IMPORTANT GAP IN ALCOHOL RESEARCH by addressing a neglected and stigmatized population from a feminist perspective.... AN APPEALING SUPPLEMENTAL TEXT for those teaching and taking alcohol and substance abuse-related courses or seminars.... A unique fusion of diverse and compelling methodologies that are often separated in the substance abuse field."

Tammy L. Anderson, PhD
*Associate Professor
Department of Sociology
and Criminal Justice
University of Delaware*

More pre-publication
REVIEWS, COMMENTARIES, EVALUATIONS...

"THIS IS THE BOOK THAT WE IN THE SUBSTANCE ABUSE TREATMENT AND RESEARCH FIELDS HAVE BEEN WAITING FOR. It fills a gaping gap in the literature, as previous studies have failed to differentiate between lesbians and gay men. The variety of methodologies, an intriguing personal narrative, and a wealth of empirically based research make this collection THE DEFINITIVE STUDY TO DATE ON LESBIANS AND SUBSTANCE ABUSE ISSUES."

Katherine van Wormer, PhD, MSSW
*Professor of Social Work
University of Northern Iowa
and Co-author of* Addiction Treatment: A Strengths Perspective

"TIMELY.... Leading researchers in the field address diverse topic areas.... This text is GROUNDBREAKING in its inclusion of sexual minority women whose voices are not customarily heard in lesbian health research, such as homeless injecting drug users. By including heterogeneous lesbian communities, this INSIGHTFUL book develops our knowledge about patterns of use among different groups. This book challenges some of the preconceptions about lesbians' use of substances, such as the absence of a 'maturing out' trend in their use of alcohol. The findings can be used to introduce organizational changes in treatment services that are sensitive to lesbians' needs."

Julie Fish, PhD
*Senior Lecturer and Research Fellow in Social Work
De Montfort University*

More pre-publication
REVIEWS, COMMENTARIES, EVALUATIONS...

"Multidisciplinary.... PROVIDES A CLEAR AND COMPELLING PICTURE OF THE PREVALENCE AND IMPACT OF SUBSTANCE USE AND MISUSE AMONG LESBIANS AND WHAT IT IS LIKE FOR THEM TO EXPERIENCE TREATMENT SERVICES.... Very well written.... Each chapter has something to say and will be appreciated differently by the wide range of readers for whom this collection has value.... Worth reading as a whole, for the story told is an important one which gains in strength with each succeeding chapter."

Susanne MacGregor, PhD
Professor of Social Policy
Department of Public Health and Policy
London School of Hygiene and Tropical Medicine

"IMPORTANT.... The authors outline the link between depression and alcohol use, the problems stemming from the lack of identity measures in population-based studies, and the fact that race, ethnicity, and age significantly influence lesbians' alcohol use."

Sheigla Murphy, PhD
Director, Center for Substance Abuse Studies
Institute for Scientific Analysis
San Francisco

Harrington Park Press

Making Lesbians Visible in the Substance Use Field

Making Lesbians Visible in the Substance Use Field has been co-published simultaneously as *Journal of Lesbian Studies*, Volume 9, Number 3 2005.

> # Monographic Separates from the *Journal of Lesbian Studies*
>
> For additional information on these and other Haworth Press titles, including descriptions, tables of contents, reviews, and prices, use the QuickSearch catalog at http://www.HaworthPress.com.

Making Lesbians Visible in the Substance Use Field, edited by Elizabeth Ettorre (Vol. 9, No. 3, 2005). *"This is the book that we in the substance abuse treatment and research fields have been waiting for." (Katherine van Wormer, PhD, MSSW, Professor of Social Work, University of Iowa; co-author,* Addiction Treatment: A Strengths Perspective*)*

Lesbian Communities: Festivals, RVs, and the Internet, edited by Esther Rothblum and Penny Sablove (Vol. 9, No. 1/2, 2005). *"Important. . . . Challenging and compelling. . . . A fascinating assortment of diverse perspectives on just what defines a lesbian 'community,' what needs and desires they meet, and how those worlds intersect with other groups and cultures." (Diane Anderson-Minshall, Executive Editor,* Curve *Magazine)*

Lesbian Ex-Lovers: The Really Long-Term Relationhips, edited by Jacqueline S. Weinstock and Esther D. Rothblum (Vol. 8, No. 3/4, 2004). *"Compelling. . . . In these heady days of legal gay marriage, this book is a good reminder of the devotion lesbians have always had to the women we've loved, and the vows we've made with our hearts, long before we demanded licenses. This book is a tribute to the long memory we have of the women's hands who have touched our most vulnerable parts, and the invisible hands that outlast our divorces." (Arlene Istar Lev, CSW-R, CSAC, Author of* Transgender Emergence *and* The Complete Lesbian and Gay Parenting Guide; *Founder and Clinical Director, Choices Counseling and Consulting)*

Lesbians, Feminism, and Psychoanalysis: The Second Wave, edited by Judith M. Glassgold and Suzanne Iasenza (Vol. 8, No. 1/2, 2004). *"This book is the first to set the tone for a lesbian psychoanalytic revolution." (Dany Nobus, PhD, Senior Lecturer in Psychology and Psychoanalytic Studies, Brunel University, United Kingdom)*

Trauma, Stress, and Resilence Among Sexual Minority Women: Rising Like the Phoenix, edited by Kimberly F. Balsam, PhD (Vol. 7, No. 4, 2003). *Provides a first-hand look at the victimization experiences that lesbian and bisexual women face as well as how they work through these challenges and emerge resilient.*

Latina Lesbian Writers and Artists, edited by María Dolores Costa, PhD (Vol. 7, No. 3, 2003). *"A fascinating journey through the Latina lesbian experience. It brings us stories of exile, assimilation, and conflict of cultures. The book takes us to the Midwest, New York, Chicana Borderlands, Mexico, Argentina, and Spain. It succeeds at showing the diversity within the Latina lesbian experience through deeply feminist testimonials of life and struggle." (Susana Cook, performance artist and playwright)*

Lesbian Rites: Symbolic Acts and the Power of Community, edited by Ramona Faith Oswald, PhD (Vol. 7, No. 2, 2003). *"Informative, enlightening, and well written . . . illuminates the range of lesbian ritual behavior in a creative and thorough manner. Ramona Faith Oswald and the contributors to this book have done scholars and students of ritual studies an important service by demonstrating the power, pervasiveness, and performative nature of lesbian ritual practices." (Cele Otnes, PhD, Associate Professor, Department of Business Administration, University of Illinois)*

Mental Health Issues for Sexual Minority Women: Redefining Women's Mental Health, edited by Tonda L. Hughes, RN, PhD, FAAN, Carrol Smith, RN, MS, and Alice Dan, PhD (Vol. 7, No. 1, 2003). *A rare look at mental health issues for lesbians and other sexual minority women.*

Addressing Homophobia and Heterosexism on College Campuses, edited by Elizabeth P. Cramer, PhD (Vol. 6, No. 3/4, 2002). *A practical guide to creating LGBT-supportive environments on college campuses.*

Femme/Butch: New Considerations of the Way We Want to Go, edited by Michelle Gibson and Deborah T. Meem (Vol. 6, No. 2, 2002). *"Disrupts the fictions of heterosexual norms. . . . A much-needed examiniation of the ways that butch/femme identitites subvert both* *heteronormativity and 'expected' lesbian behavior."* (Patti Capel Swartz, PhD, Assistant Professor of English, Kent State University)

Lesbian Love and Relationships, edited by Suzanna M. Rose, PhD (Vol. 6, No. 1, 2002). *"Suzanna Rose's collection of 13 essays is well suited to prompting serious contemplation and discussion about lesbian lives and how they are–or are not–different from others. . . . Interesting and useful for debunking some myths, confirming others, and reaching out into new territories that were previously unexplored."* (Lisa Keen, BA, MFA, Senior Political Correspondent, Washington Blade)

Everyday Mutinies: Funding Lesbian Activism, edited by Nanette K. Gartrell, MD, and Esther D. Rothblum, PhD (Vol. 5, No. 3, 2001). *"Any lesbian who fears she'll never find the money, time, or support for her work can take heart from the resourcefulness and dogged determination of the contributors to this book. Not only do these inspiring stories provide practical tips on making dreams come true, they offer an informal history of lesbian political activism since World War II."* (Jane Futcher, MA, Reporter, Marin Independent Journal, *and author of* Crush, Dream Lover, *and* Promise Not to Tell)

Lesbian Studies in Aotearoa/New Zealand, edited by Alison J. Laurie (Vol. 5, No. 1/2, 2001). *These fascinating studies analyze topics ranging from the gender transgressions of women passing as men in order to work and marry as they wished to the effects of coming out on modern women's health.*

Lesbian Self-Writing: The Embodiment of Experience, edited by Lynda Hall, PhD (Vol. 4, No. 4, 2000). *"Probes the intersection of love for words and love for women. . . . Luminous, erotic, evocative."* (Beverly Burch, PhD, psychotherapist and author, Other Women: Lesbian/Bisexual Experience and Psychoanalytic Views of Women *and* On Intimate Terms: The Psychology of Difference in Lesbian Relationships)

'Romancing the Margins'? Lesbian Writing in the 1990s, edited by Gabriele Griffin, PhD (Vol. 4, No. 2, 2000). *Explores lesbian issues through the mediums of books, movies, and poetry and offers readers critical essays that examine current lesbian writing and discuss how recent movements have tried to remove racist and antigay themes from literature and movies.*

From Nowhere to Everywhere: Lesbian Geographies, edited by Gill Valentine, PhD (Vol. 4, No. 1, 2000). *"A significant and worthy contribution to the ever growing literature on sexuality and space. . . . A politically significant volume representing the first major collection on lesbian geographies. . . . I will make extensive use of this book in my courses on social and cultural geography and sexuality and space."* (Jon Binnie, PhD, Lecturer in Human Geography, Liverpool, John Moores University, United Kingdom)

Lesbians, Levis and Lipstick: The Meaning of Beauty in Our Lives, edited by Jeanine C. Cogan, PhD, and Joanie M. Erickson (Vol. 3, No. 4, 1999). *Explores lesbian beauty norms and the effects these norms have on lesbian women.*

Lesbian Sex Scandals: Sexual Practices, Identities, and Politics, edited by Dawn Atkins, MA (Vol. 3, No. 3, 1999). *"Grounded in material practices, this collection explores confrontation and coincidence among identity politics, 'scandalous' sexual practices, and queer theory and feminism. . . . It expands notions of lesbian identification and lesbian community."* (Maria Pramaggiore, PhD, Assistant Professor, Film Studies, North Carolina State University, Raleigh)

The Lesbian Polyamory Reader: Open Relationships, Non-Monogamy, and Casual Sex, edited by Marcia Munson and Judith P. Stelboum, PhD (Vol. 3, No. 1/2, 1999). *"Offers reasonable, logical, and persuasive explanations for a style of life I had not seriously considered before. . . . A terrific read."* (Beverly Todd, Acquisitions Librarian, Estes Park Public Library, Estes Park, Colorado)

Living "Difference": Lesbian Perspectives on Work and Family Life, edited by Gillian A. Dunne, PhD (Vol. 2, No. 4, 1998). *"A fascinating, groundbreaking collection. . . . Students and professionals in psychiatry, psychology, sociology, and anthropology will find this work extremely useful and thought provoking."* (Nanette K. Gartrell, MD, Associate Clinical Professor of Psychiatry, University of California at San Francisco Medical School)

Acts of Passion: Sexuality, Gender, and Performance, edited by Nina Rapi, MA, and Maya Chowdhry, MA (Vol. 2, No. 2/3, 1998). *"This significant and impressive publication draws together a diversity of positions, practices, and polemics in relation to postmodern lesbian performance and puts them firmly on the contemporary cultural map."* (Lois Keidan, Director of Live Arts, Institute of Contemporary Arts, London, United Kingdom)

ALL HARRINGTON PARK PRESS BOOKS
AND JOURNALS ARE PRINTED
ON CERTIFIED ACID-FREE PAPER

Making Lesbians Visible in the Substance Use Field

Elizabeth Ettorre
Editor

Making Lesbians Visible in the Substance Use Field has been co-published simultaneously as *Journal of Lesbian Studies*, Volume 9, Number 3 2005.

Harrington Park Press®
An Imprint of The Haworth Press, Inc.

Published by

Harrington Park Press®, 10 Alice Street, Binghamton, NY 13904-1580 USA

Harrington Park Press® is an imprint of The Haworth Press, Inc., 10 Alice Street, Binghamton, NY 13904-1580 USA.

Making Lesbians Visible in the Substance Use Field has been co-published simultaneously as *Journal of Lesbian Studies*, Volume 9, Number 3 2005.

© 2005 by The Haworth Press, Inc. All rights reserved. No part of this work may be reproduced or utilized in any form or by any means, electronic or mechanical, including photocopying, microfilm and recording, or by any information storage and retrieval system, without permission in writing from the publisher. Printed in the United States of America.

The development, preparation, and publication of this work has been undertaken with great care. However, the publisher, employees, editors, and agents of The Haworth Press and all imprints of The Haworth Press, Inc., including The Haworth Medical Press® and The Pharmaceutical Products Press®, are not responsible for any errors contained herein or for consequences that may ensue from use of materials or information contained in this work. Opinions expressed by the author(s) are not necessarily those of The Haworth Press, Inc. With regard to case studies, identities and circumstances of individuals discussed herein have been changed to protect confidentiality. Any resemblance to actual persons, living or dead, is entirely coincidental.

Cover design by Lora Wiggins

Cover image © 2005 Andee Rudloff (www.chicNhair.com)

Library of Congress Cataloging-in-Publication Data

Making lesbians visible in the substance use field / Elizabeth Ettorre, editor.
    p. cm.
  "Co-published simultaneously as Journal of lesbian studies, volume 9, number 3, 2005."
  Includes bibliographical references and index.
  ISBN-13: 978-1-56023-616-0 (hard cover : alk. paper)
  ISBN-10: 1-56023-616-7 (hard cover : alk. paper)
  ISBN-13: 978-1-56023-617-7 (soft cover : alk. paper)
  ISBN-10: 1-56023-617-5 (soft cover : alk. paper)
  1. Lesbians–Alcohol use. 2. Lesbians–Substance use. 3. Depression in women. 4. Heterosexism. 5. Lesbians–Mental health services. I. Ettorre, Elizabeth.
HV5139.M35 2005
362.29'086'643–dc22
                                                                                        2005011229

Indexing, Abstracting & Website/Internet Coverage

This section provides you with a list of major indexing & abstracting services and other tools for bibliographic access. That is to say, each service began covering this periodical during the year noted in the right column. Most Websites which are listed below have indicated that they will either post, disseminate, compile, archive, cite or alert their own Website users with research-based content from this work. (This list is as current as the copyright date of this publication.)

Abstracting, Website/Indexing Coverage . . . . Year When Coverage Began

- *Abstracts in Social Gerontology: Current Literature on Aging* 1997

- *Business Source Corporate: coverage of nearly 3,350 quality magazines and journals; designed to meet the diverse information needs of corporations; EBSCO Publishing <http://www.epnet.com/corporate/bsource.asp>* 2002

- *Contemporary Women's Issues* 1998

- *EBSCOhost Electronic Journals Service (EJS) <http://ejournals.ebsco.com>* 2001

- *e-psyche, LLC <http://www.e-psyche.net>* 2001

- *Family & Society Studies Worldwide <http://www.nisc.com>* 2001

- *Family Index Database <http://www.familyscholar.com>* 2003

- *Feminist Periodicals: A Current Listing of Contents* 1997

- *GenderWatch <http://www.slinfo.com>* 1999

- *GLBT Life, EBSCO Publishing <http://www.epnet.com/academic/glbt.asp>* 2004

(continued)

- *Google* <http://www.google.com> 2004
- *Google Scholar* <http://www.scholar.google.com> 2004
- *Haworth Document Delivery Center*
  <http://www.HaworthPress.com/journals/dds.asp> 1997
- *HOMODOK/"Relevant" Bibliographic database,
  Documentation Centre for Gay & Lesbian Studies,
  University of Amsterdam (selective printed abstracts
  in "Homologie" and bibliographic computer databases
  covering cultural, historical, social & political aspects)*
  <http://www.ihlia.nl/> 1997
- *IBZ International Bibliography of Periodical Literature*
  <http://www.saur.de> 2001
- *IGLSS Abstracts* <http://www.iglss.org> 2000
- *Index Medicus (National Library of Medicine) . . . (print edition
  ceased . . . see instead MEDLINE)* <http://www.nlm.nih.gov> ... 2004
- *Index to Periodical Articles Related to Law*
  <http://www.law.utexas.edu> 1997
- *Internationale Bibliographie der geistes- und
  sozialwissenschaftlichen Zeitschriftenliteratur . . . See IBZ*
  <http://www.saur.de> 2001
- *Lesbian Information Service*
  <http://www.lesbianinformationservice.org> 2003
- *Links@Ovid (via CrossRef targeted DOI links)*
  <http://www.ovid.com> 2005
- *Magazines for Libraries (Katz) . . . (see 2003 edition)* 2003
- *MEDLINE (National Library of Medicine)*
  <http://www.nlm.nih.gov> 2004
- *OCLC Public Affairs Information Service*
  <http://www.pais.org> 1997
- *Ovid Linksolver (OpenURL link resolver via CrossRef targeted
  DOI links)* <http://www.linksolver.com> 2005
- *Psychological Abstracts (PsycINFO)* <http://www.apa.org> 2001
- *Psychology Today* 1999
- *PubMed* <http://www.ncbi.nlm.nih.gov/pubmed/> 2004
- *Referativnyi Zhurnal (Abstracts Journal of the All-Russian Institute
  of Scientific and Technical Information–in Russian)*
  <http://www.viniti.ru> 1997

(continued)

- *Sexual Diversity Studies: Gay, Lesbian, Bisexual & Transgender Abstracts (formerly Gay & Lesbian Abstracts) provides comprehensive & in-depth coverage of the world's GLBT literature compiled by NISC & published on the Internet & CD-ROM <http://www.nisc.com>* 2003
- *Social Services Abstracts <http://www.csa.com>* 1998
- *Sociological Abstracts (SA) <http://www.csa.com>* 1998
- *Studies on Women and Gender Abstracts <http://www.tandf.co.uk/swa>* 1998
- *zetoc <http://zetoc.mimas.ac.uk>* 2004

Special Bibliographic Notes related to special journal issues (separates) and indexing/abstracting:

- indexing/abstracting services in this list will also cover material in any "separate" that is co-published simultaneously with Haworth's special thematic journal issue or DocuSerial. Indexing/abstracting usually covers material at the article/chapter level.
- monographic co-editions are intended for either non-subscribers or libraries which intend to purchase a second copy for their circulating collections.
- monographic co-editions are reported to all jobbers/wholesalers/approval plans. The source journal is listed as the "series" to assist the prevention of duplicate purchasing in the same manner utilized for books-in-series.
- to facilitate user/access services all indexing/abstracting services are encouraged to utilize the co-indexing entry note indicated at the bottom of the first page of each article/chapter/contribution.
- this is intended to assist a library user of any reference tool (whether print, electronic, online, or CD-ROM) to locate the monographic version if the library has purchased this version but not a subscription to the source journal.
- individual articles/chapters in any Haworth publication are also available through the Haworth Document Delivery Service (HDDS).

ABOUT THE EDITOR

Elizabeth Ettorre, PhD, was born in Bridgeport, Connecticut, USA, and came to England in 1972 upon completion of her BA in sociology at Fordham University, New York. After finishing her PhD in sociology at the London School of Economics and Political Science in 1978, she was a research sociologist at the Institute of Psychiatry, Addiction Research Unit. After seven years at the Institute, she went on to the Department of Politics and Sociology, Birkbeck College, and then on to Charing Cross Medical School's Centre for Drugs and Health Behaviour, where she continued her research in the sociology of addiction. In 1991, she left England to work at Abo Academy University in Turku, Finland, with Professor Elianne Riska on a study on gender and psychotropic drugs. In March 1998, she returned to the UK to the Department of Sociology at the University of Plymouth. Currently, she is Professor of Sociology and Associate Dean (Research and Enterprise), Faculty of Social Science and Business at Plymouth. She holds honorary academics posts in Finland as a Docent in Sociology at Abo Academy University and University of Helsinki, in the USA at the Institute for Scientific Analysis, San Francisco, and in the UK at EGenis, ESRC Centre for Genomics in Society, University of Exeter. Elizabeth has had a consistent research interest in women and substance use and gender and health and has published widely. Besides numerous journal articles, her books include: *Lesbians, Women and Society* (1980); *Women and Substance Use* (1992); *Gendered Moods* (1995) with Elianne Riska; *Women and Alcohol: A Private Pleasure or a Public Problem?* (1997); *Reproductive Genetics, Gender and the Body* (2002); *Before Birth* (2001) and *Revisioning Women and Drug Use* (forthcoming). Professor Ettorre lives with her partner, Imma, in Truro, Cornwall.

Making Lesbians Visible
in the Substance Use Field

CONTENTS

Introduction: Making Lesbians Visible in the Substance Use Field 1
   Elizabeth Ettorre

The Co-Occurrence of Depression and Alcohol Dependence
   Symptoms in a Community Sample of Lesbians 7
      Wendy B. Bostwick
      Tonda L. Hughes
      Timothy Johnson

Alcohol Consumption, Alcohol-Related Problems, and Other
   Substance Use Among Lesbian and Bisexual Women 19
      Laurie Drabble
      Karen Trocki

Alcohol Use and Alcohol-Related Problems in Self-Identified
   Lesbians: An Historical Cohort Analysis 31
      Cheryl A. Parks
      Tonda L. Hughes

Substance Use and Social Identity in the Lesbian Community 45
      Molly Kerby
      Richard Wilson
      Thomas Nicholson
      John B. White

Toward a Grounded Theory of Lesbians' Recovery
 from Addiction   57
   Connie R. Matthews
   Peggy Lorah
   Jaime Fenton

Labelling Out: The Personal Account
 of an Ex-Alcoholic Lesbian Feminist   69
   Patsy Staddon

Lesbian, Gay, and Bisexual Clients' Experiences in Treatment
 for Addiction   79
   Connie R. Matthews
   Mary M. D. Selvidge

Predicting, Understanding and Changing: Three Research
 Paradigms Regarding Alcohol Use Among Lesbians   91
   Maria Pettinato

Exploring an HIV Paradox: An Ethnography of Sexual Minority
 Women Injectors   103
   Rebecca M. Young
   Samuel R. Friedman
   Patricia Case

Index   117

Introduction:
Making Lesbians Visible in the Substance Use Field

Elizabeth Ettorre

Over the past thirty-five years, I have been working in the substance use field where I have met many lesbian substance users. I uphold the viewpoint that lesbians are an invisible minority and that creating affirmative healing environments is a commitment to generating visibility and acknowledging lesbians' value as a group (Underhill & Osterman, 1991). If we are to recognize fully the complex processes involved in managing the dual identities of lesbian and substance user, we need to become advocates of culturally competent services (Finnegan & McNally, 2002). Viewpoints such as these motivated this volume. The papers bring together quantitative, qualitative, ethnographic, theoretical and autobiographical approaches to lesbians and substance use. While risk of substance use, as a significant characteristic of lesbian health, has more often than not been ignored (Gay and Lesbian Medical Association, 2001; Solarz, 1999), every author highlights how a lesbian sensitive perspective on lesbian health, in general, and lesbian substance use, in particular, can shed new light on this neglected research area, as well as illuminate important areas of concern for treaters and researchers alike.

[Haworth co-indexing entry note]: "Introduction: Making Lesbians Visible in the Substance Use Field." Ettorre, Elizabeth. Co-published simultaneously in *Journal of Lesbian Studies* (Harrington Park Press, an imprint of The Haworth Press, Inc.) Vol. 9, No. 3, 2005, pp. 1-5; and: *Making Lesbians Visible in the Substance Use Field* (ed: Elizabeth Ettorre) Harrington Park Press, an imprint of The Haworth Press, Inc., 2005, pp. 1-5. Single or multiple copies of this article are available for a fee from The Haworth Document Delivery Service [1-800-HAWORTH, 9:00 a.m. - 5:00 p.m. (EST). E-mail address: docdelivery@haworthpress.com].

Available online at http://www.haworthpress.com/web/JLS
© 2005 by The Haworth Press, Inc. All rights reserved.
doi:10.1300/J155v09n03_01

One key area of concern relates to understanding the complexities of the relationship between sexual orientation and substance use. While all papers touch upon this issue, four papers address it specifically. For example, the paper by Wendy Bostwick, Tonda Hughes and Timothy Johnson explores the link between depression and alcohol use disorders in lesbians and the complexities of substance use as a predictor for the incidence of depression. Using data from the Chicago Health and Life Experiences of Women Study (CHLEW), they examine the prevalence of lifetime and past year depression and past year alcohol dependence symptoms in a large community-based sample of self-identified lesbians. The influence of depression on lesbian alcohol use was found to be both constant and powerful. This work reveals the value of research that focuses on sexual minority women and calls for a more concerted effort to better understand how social factors, in particular stigma and bigotry, can have a negative influence on the mental health outcomes of lesbians.

Lesbians and bisexual women appear to have infinitely bigger odds for reporting alcohol dependence and alcohol-related consequences. Laurie Drabble and Karen Trocki's work alludes to this finding, as they recognize the importance of disaggregating populations of women that are often combined (i.e., self-identified lesbians, bisexuals, heterosexual women who have had same sex partners) in population based studies related to alcohol, drugs and mental health. They report on data from the 2000 National Alcohol Survey and show that among sexual orientation groups, substance use patterns were multifaceted as well as wide-ranging. Their work indicates that including measures of sexual orientation and identity is necessary if we are to have a clear picture of variations in substance use risks between the different sexual orientation categories of women.

Using data from the above mentioned CHLEW study, Cheryl Parks and Tonda Hughes contend that race/ethnicity and age linked with historical context (including young, 'Rights,' middle-aged, 'Liberation' and older, 'Stonewall' cohorts) will have significant influences on lesbians' alcohol use. Their findings that high rates of lifetime and current drinking, high rates of lifetime heavy drinking and other problem-drinking indicators such as treatment for alcohol-related problems support the depiction of lesbians as being at risk for alcohol-related health problems. The authors found hardly any differences in levels of alcohol use or drinking-related problems across race/ethnic groups. However, their findings suggest a somewhat higher risk for problems among older Black and younger White and Hispanic lesbians. While heterosexual women may experience a "maturing out" of drinking, this appears less clear for lesbians. Most importantly, they contend that the absence of age-related declines found in previous studies may be a result of restricted age ranges of study samples.

Molly Kerby, Richard Wilson, Thomas Nicholson, and John White found that lesbians with higher self-esteem and a more positive social identity tend to use alcohol, tobacco and other drugs more frequently. Their findings suggest that these individuals may be more likely to frequent lesbian bars and network in the lesbian culture. While the authors imply that alcohol, tobacco and other drug use in the lesbian community is complicated, they contend that it is inadequate to approach simply the issue of substance use. The suggestion is that programs designed specifically for lesbians must include the varied and numerous causes of substance use.

In the current volume, three papers focus specifically on recovery and treatment. The importance of self-acceptance in recovery for lesbians emerged as the crucial, observable finding (associated to the link between sexual orientation and addiction) for Connie Matthews, Peggy Lorah and Jaime Fenton, albeit they did not speak directly to this issue in their study. The authors contend that lesbians need treatment and support systems which value both their sexual orientation and addiction. Attention needs to be given to the identities (i.e., gender, sexual orientation, ethnicity, and addiction) most salient for lesbians in recovery at any one time as well as the sorts of experiences they have had with stigma and discrimination. Given that self-acceptance is crucial for developing sobriety, lesbians in recovery need to deal with their own internalized homophobia and the shame associated with it. Some lesbians will learn to redefine spirituality, an important element in recovery, but it is important that this process is flexible. For example, lesbians in treatment should not feel compelled to accept a Christian god as the basis of their spirituality.

Patsy Staddon looks at the importance of self-acceptance through her own experience as a lesbian alcoholic who went through alcohol treatment. She traces her development through a sociological perspective and sees herself as a lesbian who has been wounded through engagement with the heternormative society in which she grew up. Drinking alcohol was a way of coping when she felt that she did not fit in. Looking critically at alcohol treatment, she contrasts what lesbians want from treatment with treatment as it often is for lesbians. She discards the disease model, including AA's, and the view that a recovering alcoholic is always in recovery. For her, self-acceptance was a key factor in her own recovery. For example, once she was able to accept herself in a supportive community of women, she could look seriously at herself and stop drinking.

Studying lesbian, gay, and bisexual clients' treatment experiences, Connie Matthews and Mary Selvidge suggest that more can be done by addiction counselors and treatment facilities to address the recovery needs of these clients. For example, they want addiction counselors and treaters to be proactive. More effort could be put into hiring openly Lesbian, Gay, and Bisexual (LGB) counselors. The value of this strategy is that LGB counselors will be positive role models for LGB clients in treatment and enhance the healing process.

A final theme explored is that of marginalization. Marginalization of lesbian research on the research funding front is important for Maria Pettinato who appeals to all researchers in this field to recognize the value in asking, How can we predict?, How can we understand?, and How can we change? These questions reflect Empirical Post Positivist, Interpretive, and Critical Social research paradigms, respectively. For Pettinato, defining one's research paradigm plays a crucial role in obtaining funding for research. She recognizes that while lesbian health may be an emerging area of research, it does not have funding priority. Nevertheless, future research agendas and funding priorities should include all three valuable paradigms. To be respectful towards and indeed to use all paradigms is an important way for research on minority populations, such as lesbian substance users, to develop in an appropriate way.

The study presented by Rebecca Young, Samuel Friedman and Patricia Case suggests that experiences of manifold marginalization are the most probable justification for sexual minority women injectors' heightened HIV risks and infection in comparison to other drug injectors. Looking at sexual minority injectors through the lens of structural and political intersectionality, they contend that research and policy on women drug users and HIV/AIDS tend to position sexual minority women injectors as a marginal group. In fact, sexual minority women injectors should be the key focus as these women remain at highest risk in both areas.

In conclusion, this volume is an important step in helping to create an environment in which the hurt of invisibility of lesbian substance users can begin to be healed. In recent work, I debate how we can move forward and become more gender sensitive especially to women who have been the traditional underdogs in the substance use field (Ettorre, 2004). In looking specifically at lesbian substance users, we need to choose intentionally how we will transform obsolete ideas, beliefs and practices as we construct 'lesbian sensitive' perspectives. I am hopeful that this type of work will be ongoing and that we can be generous to those lesbians we research and treat.

REFERENCES

Ettorre, E. (2004) 'Revisioning women and drug use: gender sensitivity, gendered bodies and reducing harm'. *International Journal of Drugs Policy, 15, 5-6: 327-335.*

Finnegan, D. G. & McNally, E. B. (2002) *Counselling lesbian, gay, bisexual, and transgender substance users: dual identities.* New York: The Haworth Press.

Gay and Lesbian Medical Association. (2001). *Healthy People 2010: A Companion Document.*

Solarz, A. (ed.) (1999) *Lesbian Health: Current Assessment and Directions for the Future.* Washington, DC: National Academy Press.

Underhill, B. L. & Osterman, S. E. (1991) 'The Pain of Invisibility: Issues for lesbians': In. P. Roth (ed.), *Alcohol and drugs are women's issues* (Volume 1: Review of the Issues). Metuchen, New Jersey and London: Women's Action Alliance and The Scarecrow Press.

The Co-Occurrence of Depression and Alcohol Dependence Symptoms in a Community Sample of Lesbians

Wendy B. Bostwick
Tonda L. Hughes
Timothy Johnson

SUMMARY. Numerous studies have found an association between depression and alcohol use disorders in women. Little is known, however, about the relationship between depression and alcohol use among lesbians. We examined the prevalence of depression and alcohol dependence

---

Wendy B. Bostwick, MPH, PhD (cand.), is a doctoral candidate in public health, University of Illinois at Chicago. Her research interests include bisexual women's health, the measurement of sexual orientation, and social determinants of health. Tonda L. Hughes, PhD, RN, FAAN, is Associate Professor in the Department of Public Health, Mental Health and Administrative Nursing, University of Illinois at Chicago. She is also Director of Research at UIC's National Center of Excellence in Women's Health. Timothy Johnson, PhD, is the Director of the UIC Survey Research Laboratory. He also holds a joint appointment as Professor in Public Administration and Research Professor in Public Health, University of Illinois at Chicago.

Address correspondence to: Wendy Bostwick, University of Michigan Substance Abuse Research Center, 202 S Traverwood Dr., Suite C, Ann Arbor, MI 48105.

The development of this manuscript was supported by a National Research Service Award T32 DA 07293 (Bostwick) from the National Institute on Drug Abuse, National Institutes of Health and from the National Institute of Alcohol Abuse and Alcoholism (R01 #AA13228, Hughes).

[Haworth co-indexing entry note]: "The Co-Occurrence of Depression and Alcohol Dependence Symptoms in a Community Sample of Lesbians." Bostwick, Wendy B., Tonda L. Hughes, and Timothy Johnson. Co-published simultaneously in *Journal of Lesbian Studies* (Harrington Park Press, an imprint of The Haworth Press, Inc.) Vol. 9, No. 3, 2005, pp. 7-18; and: *Making Lesbians Visible in the Substance Use Field* (ed: Elizabeth Ettorre) Harrington Park Press, an imprint of The Haworth Press, Inc., 2005, pp. 7-18. Single or multiple copies of this article are available for a fee from The Haworth Document Delivery Service [1-800-HAWORTH, 9:00 a.m. - 5:00 p.m. (EST). E-mail address: docdelivery@haworthpress.com].

Available online at http://www.haworthpress.com/web/JLS
© 2005 by The Haworth Press, Inc. All rights reserved.
doi:10.1300/J155v09n03_02

symptoms as well as the co-occurrence of these two health problems in a large community-based sample of women who self-identified as lesbian. Past year alcohol dependence symptoms were significantly associated with both past year and lifetime depression. Lifetime depression was higher among White and Latina lesbians than among African American lesbians. Younger women and those not currently in a committed relationship more commonly reported past year depression. Younger age was the strongest predictor of the co-occurrence of depression and alcohol dependence symptoms. *[Article copies available for a fee from The Haworth Document Delivery Service: 1-800-HAWORTH. E-mail address: <docdelivery@haworthpress.com> Website: <http://www.HaworthPress.com> © 2005 by The Haworth Press, Inc. All rights reserved.]*

KEYWORDS. Depression, alcohol dependence, lesbian, co-morbidity, sexual identity, sexual orientation

INTRODUCTION

According to reports from the United States Surgeon General, in any given year, about 28% of the adult population has either a mental health or addictive disorder and 3% have both disorders simultaneously (USDHHS, 1999). In order to effectively address the myriad issues related to co-morbid substance use and mental health disorders, it is necessary to understand which disorders are most likely to co-occur and among which populations. To this end, both clinical and community-based studies have found that the co-occurrence of depression and alcohol disorders is much more common in women than men (Dixit & Crum, 2000; Grant & Harford, 1995; Hesselbrock & Hesselbrock, 1997; Kessler et al., 1997). Despite the well-established link between depression and alcohol use disorders in women, almost no research has examined this relationship in lesbians.

Sexual minority women share many of the same health risks as women in the general population; however, their status as part of a stigmatized minority group is believed to increase their risk for certain health problems or health risk behaviors (Meyer, 2003). In particular, exposure to discrimination, heterosexism and homophobia may contribute to mental health problems such as depression and anxiety, and may also heighten risk for substance use and abuse among lesbian, gay and bisexual populations (Brooks, 1981; DiPlacido, 1998; Meyer, 1995).

Given findings suggesting that women who identify as lesbians may be at heightened risk for both depression (Diamant & Wold, 2003; Matthews, Hughes, Johnson, Razzano & Cassidy, 2002; Oetjen & Rothblum, 2000) and alcohol use disorders (Hughes, Wilsnack & Johnson, in press; McKirnan & Peterson, 1989; Meyer, 2003; Skinner & Otis, 1996), studies of co-morbidity may be especially relevant for this population of women.

We examined the prevalence of lifetime and past year depression and past year alcohol dependence symptoms in a large community-based sample of self-identified lesbians. In addition, we explored the co-occurrence of depression and alcohol dependence symptoms controlling for socio-demographic correlates.

METHODS

Sampling and Recruitment

Data are from the first wave of the Chicago Health and Life Experiences of Women (CHLEW) study conducted in 2000-2001. Women who self-identified as lesbian, were English speaking, and were 18 years old or older were recruited using a broad variety of sources (bars were excluded). Recruitment efforts targeted racial/ethnic minority and other hard-to-reach women (e.g., older lesbians and those with lower incomes). All participants were interviewed either in their homes, or in another private location of their choosing, by a trained, female interviewer. A $35 incentive was offered to all participants.

Respondents were screened for eligibility using the question "Understanding that sexual identity is only one part of your identity do you consider yourself to be lesbian, bisexual, heterosexual, transgender, or something else?" Despite the fact that women who did not identify as lesbian during screening were excluded, 11 participants identified as bisexual in the study interview, one identified as "queer" and another refused to be labeled. These women were compared with the rest of the sample on demographic characteristics other than sexual orientation. No statistically significant differences were found, and they were included in the analyses.

Survey Instrument

Respondents were interviewed in person using the National Study of Health and Life Experiences of Women (HLEW) questionnaire (see, e.g., Wilsnack, Klassen, Shur, & Wilsnack, 1991; Wilsnack, Wilsnack, Kristjanson, & Harris, 1998). The HLEW questionnaire has been developed over the past 20 years and has been used in five waves of data collection in a longitudinal study of the drinking behavior and drinking-related problems of almost 2000 women. Following pretests, slight modifications in the wording of some questions were made to the HLEW for the Chicago study (CHLEW) to improve sensitivity to, and inclusiveness of, lesbians' experiences.

Measures

Alcohol Dependence Symptoms

Five questions about alcohol dependence symptoms drawn from indices used in previous national drinking surveys included: (1) memory lapses while drinking (blackouts); (2) morning drinking; (3) rapid drinking; (4) inability to stop drinking before becoming intoxicated; and (5) inability to stop or reduce alcohol consumption over time. These questions were selected to assess the diversity of alcohol-related problems and symptoms experienced by women drinkers in the general population and are not used diagnostically. A dichotomous measure (any/no past year alcohol dependence symptoms) was constructed.

Depression

We assessed depression using questions from the Diagnostic Interview Schedule that approximate a clinical diagnosis (based on Diagnostic and Statistical Manual of Mental Disorders criteria, Ed. III, APA, 1980). Respondents were asked about 21 symptoms–such as feeling tired out all the time, trouble with sleeping, and appetite changes–and whether they had experienced these symptoms for two weeks or more. Those who reported three or more symptoms that persisted for two or more weeks and included depressed mood or loss of pleasure and interest were considered to have met criteria for a depressive episode. Responses to a question about when the last episode of depression ended were used to construct lifetime and 12-month depression measures.

Socio-Demographic Characteristics

Measures of respondent age, race/ethnicity, education, annual household income and current relationship status were examined due to evidence suggesting that these variables are correlated with depression, alcohol use or both. In bivariate analyses, age, education and income were collapsed into four categories. In all regression models, these variables were treated as continuous.

Co-Occurrence of Depression and Alcohol-Dependence Symptoms

Because questions included in the CHLEW were not sufficient to determine a diagnosis of alcohol dependence, we refer to "co-occurrence" rather than "co-morbidity." We define co-occurrence as the occurrence of a least one depressive episode and one alcohol dependence symptom within the same time frame, specifically, lifetime or past twelve months.

DATA ANALYSES

Data analyses excluded 23 women who never drank in their lifetime. Asian/Pacific Islanders, Native Americans, and those who identified as bi- or multi-racial were also excluded because group sizes were too small to permit reliable group comparisons (n = 27). The final sample equaled 403 women (lifetime abstainers and "other" racial groups were not mutually exclusive). Summary statistics were used to describe the sample. Chi-square tests were conducted to examine differences in past year dependence symptoms by lifetime and past year depression, and across demographic groups. Chi-squares were also used to examine associations between past year co-occurrence of alcohol dependence and depression and respondent demographics. Multiple logistic regression models were tested to examine the effects of (a) depressive symptoms and socio-demographic measures on past year alcohol dependence symptoms and (b) sociodemographic measures on past year alcohol dependence and depression co-occurrence. Odds ratios (OR) and 95% confidence intervals are reported for these analyses.

RESULTS

Table 1 summarizes the socio-demographic characteristics of the sample and the prevalence of depression and alcohol dependence symptoms. The majority of respondents were white (50%), had a bachelor's degree or above (56%) and were in a committed relationship (69%). Overall, 57% reported lifetime depression, 22% reported past-year depression and 27% reported having experienced at least one alcohol dependence symptom during the past year. Thirteen percent (n = 54) had

TABLE 1. Lifetime and Past Year Depression, and Past Year Alcohol Dependence Symptoms by Demographic Characteristics

	Lifetime Depression	Past Year Depression	Past Year Alcohol Dependence Symptoms	Co-Occurring Past Year Depression and Alcohol Dependence Symptoms
Total	228 (57%)	90 (22%)	106 (27%)	54 (13%)
Age				
< 30	58 (58%)	32 (32%)**	45 (45%)***	27 (27%)***
31-40	72 (58%)	33 (26%)	31 (25%)	13 (19%)
41-49	49 (52%)	13 (14%)	20 (22%)	9 (10%)
>50	49 (60%)	12 (15%)	10 (12%)	5 (6%)
Race				
African-American	56 (47%)*	26 (22%)	42 (35%)*	16 (13%)
Latina	49 (62%)	25 (32%)	21 (27%)	17 (22%)*
White	123 (61%)	39 (19%)	43 (22%)	21 (10%)
Education				
High school or less	32 (56%)	19 (33%)	17 (30%)	9 (16%)
Some college/2yr degree	74 (62%)	44 (36%)	39 (32%)	16 (12%)
Bachelor's	59 (57%)	43 (41%)	28 (27%)	19 (18%)
Graduate or professional degree	58 (48%)	33 (24%)	22 (21%)	10 (19%)
Income				
$0-$19,999	56 (57%)	42 (30%)*	40 (40%)***	20 (20%)*
$20,000-$39,999	64 (65%)	36 (26%)	28 (28%)	15 (15%)
$40,000-$74,999	67 (58%)	41 (30%)	28 (25%)	15 (13%)
$75,000 and up	41 (46%)	20 (23%)	20 (12%)	4 (5%)
Relationship Status				
In a committed relationship	143 (54%)	83 (31%)	55 (21%)	38 (14%)
Not in committed relationship	77 (64%)	50 (42%)*	45 (38%)***	30 (25%)**

*p < .05, ** p < .01, *** p < .001

co-occurring depression and alcohol dependence symptoms. Lifetime depression was significantly higher among Whites and Latinas than among African American lesbians ($\chi^2 (2, 401) = 6.67$, p = .036). Past year depression was more common in younger respondents, those not in committed relationships and those with lower household incomes. Respondents who were younger, had a lower income, were African American or who were not in a committed relationship were more likely to report past year alcohol dependence symptoms. These findings held for past year co-occurrence, with one exception: *Latinas* were significantly more likely to have co-occurring disorders ($\chi^2 (2, 403) = 6.12$, p = .047).

Associations between depression and alcohol dependence symptoms were examined in multiple logistic regression models that adjusted for socio-demographic measures (Table 2). Past year depression was found to be a risk factor for past year alcohol dependence (OR = 2.03, CI = 1.23-3.34, $p < .01$) after adjusting for socio-demographic variables. Younger age (OR = 0.95, CI = 0.92-0.97, $p < .001$) and not being in a committed relationship (OR = 1.96, CI = 1.15-3.35, $p < .01$) each increased the odds of alcohol dependence symptoms.

Lifetime depression was also a risk factor for past year alcohol dependence symptoms (OR = 1.76, CI = 1.04-2.97, $p < .05$). Women with a history of depression were nearly twice as likely as women without lifetime depression to report alcohol dependence symptoms. Younger age and not being in a committed relationship were also associated with alcohol dependence symptoms.

The relationship between socio-demographic characteristics and past year co-occurrence was next examined using logistic regression (see third equation in Table 2) and only age was found to be an independent risk factor for co-occurrence.

DISCUSSION

Similar to women in the general population, we found an association between depression and alcohol dependence symptoms in our sample of lesbian-identified women. The presence of past year depression doubled the odds of having at least one alcohol dependence symptom within the same time frame. Further, lifetime depression increased the odds of past year alcohol dependence symptoms almost two-fold, suggesting that the influence of depression on alcohol use in lesbians is both potent and persistent–a finding which has important implications for alcohol use prevention and treatment programs.

While age was the only significant predictor of co-occurrence in the regression models, a trend in the data suggested that women in committed relationships may be at lower risk for co-occurring depression and alcohol dependence. The protective health effects of being in a relationship are well documented in the public health literature (see Lillard & Panis, 1996; Waldron, Hughes & Brooks, 1996). Our findings suggest that this benefit may also be relevant for same-sex couples, although further research is needed to better address this potential protective factor among lesbian, gay, and bisexual populations.

TABLE 2. Adjusted Odds Ratios (Confidence Intervals) for Logistic Regression Models Examining Predictors of Past Year Alcohol Dependence Symptoms and Co-Occurring Past Year Depression and Alcohol Dependence Symptoms

	Past Year Alcohol Dependence Symptoms		Past Year Depression Symptoms		Co-Occurring Past Year Depression and Alcohol Dependence Symptoms	
	Odds Ratios	Confidence Intervals	Odds Ratios	Confidence Intervals	Odds Ratios	Confidence Intervals
Independent Variables						
Past Year Depression	2.03**	(1.23-3.34)	---	---	---	---
Lifetime Depression	---	---	1.76*	(1.04-2.97)	---	---
Demographic Variables						
Age (in years)	0.95***	(0.92-0.97)	0.95***	(0.92-0.97)	0.97**	(0.94-0.99)
White (contrast)	1.00	---	1.00	---	1.00	---
African American	1.61	(0.90-2.88)	1.71	(0.94-3.10)	1.04	(0.53-2.03)
Latina	0.91	(0.47-1.77)	0.97	(0.50-1.89)	1.69	(0.86-3.32)
Education	1.00	(0.75-1.32)	1.03	(0.78-1.36)	1.07	(0.79-1.45)
Income	0.83	(0.63-1.09)	0.82	(0.62-1.09)	0.82	(0.60-1.12)
In a committed relationship (contrast)	1.00	---	1.00	---	1.00	---
Not in a relationship	1.96**	(1.15-3.35)	2.04**	(1.19-3.48)	1.78	(0.99-3.21)

* p < .05, ** p < .01, *** p < .001

Finally, compared to other estimates of co-occurrence among women that range from 6.7% (Wang & El-Guebaly, 2004) to 8.3% (Grant & Harford, 1995), 13% of the women in our sample reported both depression and alcohol dependence symptoms in the past year. The higher rate of co-occurrence in our study can likely be accounted for in part by the measures used. In particular, our use of a dichotomous measure indicating one or more alcohol dependence symptom(s) is much broader than measures employed in the above studies. Thus, the finding of a higher co-occurrence should be interpreted cautiously. Future studies using more rigorous diagnostic measures are needed.

Unlike the rate of co-occurrence which was not far outside the range found in other studies, prevalence of each independent disorder among women in our sample stands in stark contrast to those of women in the general population. We found rates of depression and alcohol dependence symptoms that are more than double those for women in general. Whereas population-based rates of lifetime depression for women range from about 11% (Grant & Harford, 1995) to 21% (Kessler et al., 1994), more than one-half (57%) of our sample met the study criteria for lifetime depression. In addition, the rate of past year depression among women in our sample (22%) is two to five times higher than estimates for women in the general population (Grant & Harford, 1995; Kessler et al., 1994). Further, unlike studies of women in the general population, reports of lifetime depression in our sample *did not* decrease with age; rates for lesbians 50 years and older were slightly higher than rates for lesbians 30 years and younger.

In terms of alcohol dependence, compared with results from the HLEW, upon which the CHLEW is based, lesbians were nearly three times as likely to have experienced one or more dependence symptom in the past year–27% compared with 9.5% (Wilsnack, Wilsnack & Hiller-Sturmhofel, 1994). In particular, being younger, having lower household income and not being in a relationship were all significantly associated with past year alcohol dependence symptoms, findings similar to those reported by Wang and El Guebaly (2004).

Results support previous conclusions that lesbians are at heightened risk for poor mental health outcomes and highlight the importance of research that focuses on sexual minority populations. While both affective and substance use disorders originate from a confluence of biological, genetic, environmental and social factors, the elevated rates seen in lesbian-identified women are cause for concern. Such disparities require ongoing and concerted efforts to better understand the ways in which social determinants, particularly those related to stigma and discrimination, adversely affect health outcomes.

Limitations

Lack of a diagnostic measure of alcohol dependence limits the conclusions that can be drawn and makes it difficult to compare findings related to co-occurrence with findings about co-morbidity from general population studies. Also, our non-probability sample limits generalizability. Women who volunteered to participate may differ from those who did not in ways that are directly or indirectly related to the study variables. Women agreed to participate in CHLEW knowing that they would be asked questions about sexual orientation, as well as about a number of other potentially sensitive topics including substance use and depression. Women uncomfortable disclosing information about their alcohol use or experiences with depression were probably less likely to participate in the study. Finally, because data used in these analyses are cross-sectional, we were unable to address causality or temporal order vis-à-vis depression and alcohol dependence symptoms.

Conclusion

Despite the limitations, the findings presented here are an important addition to a growing body of research that demonstrates health disparities among sexual minority women. The high rates of depression and alcohol dependence symptoms suggest that health care providers who work with lesbians need to be mindful of these problems and the risks associated with them. In addition, given consistent associations between younger age and depression and alcohol dependence symptoms, prevention strategies and treatment programs that are tailored to younger lesbians, and women who may be questioning their sexual identity are needed.

This research is a step toward understanding depression and alcohol problems and their co-occurrence among lesbians. Future studies would be strengthened by the use of diagnostic measures of alcohol dependence, as well as data collected across multiple time points. Finally, there is a need to include measures of sexual identity in national health studies, as this will assist in creating a more thorough understanding of the complex interplay of individual behavior, socio-cultural factors and health status among sexual minority populations.

REFERENCES

American Psychiatric Association. (1980). *Diagnostic and statistical manual of mental disorders* (3rd ed.). Washington, DC: Author.

Brooks, V. R. (1981). *Minority stress and lesbian women.* Lexington, MA: Lexington Books.

Diamant, A. L., & Wold, C. (2003). Sexual orientation and variation in physical and mental health status among women. *Journal of Women's Health*, 12(3), 41-49.

DiPlacido, J. (1998b). Minority stress among lesbians, gay men, and bisexuals: A consequence of heterosexism, homophobia, and stigmatization. In G.M. Herek (Ed.), *Stigma and sexual orientation. Psychological Perspectives on Lesbian and Gay Issues*, 4 (pp. 138-159). Thousand Oaks, CA: Sage.

Dixit, A.R., & Crum, R.M. (2000). Prospective study of depression and the risk of heavy alcohol use in women. *The American Journal of Psychiatry*, 157(5), 751-758.

Grant, B.F., & Harford, T.C. (1995). Comorbidity between DSM-IV alcohol use disorders and major depression: Results of a national survey. *Drug and Alcohol Dependence*, 39, 197-206.

Hesselbrock, M.N., & Hesselbrock, V.M. (1997). Gender, alcoholism, and psychiatric comorbidity. In R.W. Wilsnack & S.C. Wilsnack (Eds.), *Gender and alcohol: Individual and Social Perspectives* (pp. 49-71). New Brunswick, NJ: Rutgers Center of Alcohol Studies.

Hughes, T.L., Wilsnack, S.C., & Johnson, T. (in press). Investigating lesbians' mental health and alcohol use: What is an appropriate comparison group?. In A. Omoto & H. Kurtzman (Eds.), *Recent research on sexual orientation, mental health, and substance use*. Washington, D.C.: American Psychological Association Books.

Kessler, R.C., Crum, R.M., Warner, L.A., Nelson, C.B, Schulenberg, J., & Anthony, J.C. (1997). Lifetime co-occurrence of DSM-III-R alcohol abuse and dependence with other psychiatric disorders in the national comorbidity survey. *Archives of General Psychiatry*, 54(4), 313-321.

Kessler, R.C., McGonagle, K.A., Zhao, S., Nelson, C.B., Hughes, M., Eshleman, S. et al (1994). Lifetime and 12-month prevalence of DSM-III-R psychiatric disorders in the United States. *Archives of General Psychiatry*, 51, 8-19.

Lillard, L.A. & Panis, C.W.A. (1996). Marital status and mortality: The role of health. *Demography*, 33, 313-327.

Matthews, A.K., Hughes, T., Johnson, T., Razzano, L., & Cassidy, R. (2002). Prediction of depression in a community based sample of healthy females: Role of sexual orientation. *American Journal of Public Health*, 92(7), 1131-1139.

McKirnan, D.J., & Peterson, P.L. (1989). Alcohol and drug use among homosexual men and women: Epidemiology and population characteristics. *Addictive Behaviors*, 14, 545-553.

Meyer, I.H. (2003). Prejudice, social stress, and mental health in lesbian, gay, and bisexual populations: Conceptual issues and research evidence. *Psychological Bulletin*, 129(5), 674-697.

Meyer, I.H. (1995). Minority stress and mental health in gay men. *Journal of Health and Social Behavior*, 7, 9-25.

Oetjen, H., & Rothblum, E. D. (2000). When lesbians aren't gay: Factors affecting depression among lesbians. *Journal of Homosexuality, 39*(1), 49-73.

Skinner, W.F., & Otis, M.D. (1996). Drug and alcohol use among lesbian and gay people in a Southern US sample: Epidemiological, comparative, and methodological findings from the trilogy project. *Journal of Homosexuality,* 30(3), 59-91.

U.S. Department of Health and Human Services. (USDHHS) (1999). *Mental Health: A Report of the Surgeon General.* Rockville, MD: U.S. Department of Health and Human Services, Substance Abuse and Mental Health Services Administration, Center for Mental Health Services, National Institutes of Health, and National Institute of Mental Health.

Wang J., & El-Guebaly, N. (2004). Sociodemographic factors associated with comorbid major depressive episodes and alcohol dependence in the general population. *Canadian Journal of Psychiatry,* 49(1), 37-44.

Waldron, I., Hughes, M.E., & Brooks, T.L. (1996). Marriage protection and marriage selection–Prospective evidence for reciprocal effects of marital status and health *Social Science & Medicine,* 43(1), 113-123.

Wilsnack, S.C., Klassen A.D., Shur, B.E, & Wilsnack, R.W. (1991). Predicting onset and chronicity of women's problem drinking: A five-year longitudinal analysis. *American Journal of Public Health,* 81, 305-318.

Wilsnack, R.W., Wilsnack, S.C., Kristjanson, A.F., & Harris, T.R. (1998). Ten-year prediction of women's drinking behavior in a nationally representative sample. *Women's Health: Research on Gender, Behavior and Policy,* 4, 199-230.

Wilsnack, S.C., Wilsnack, R.W., & Hiller-Sturmhofel, S. (1994). How women drink: Epidemiology of women's drinking and problem drinking. *Alcohol Health & Research World,* 18(3), 173-181.

Alcohol Consumption, Alcohol-Related Problems, and Other Substance Use Among Lesbian and Bisexual Women

Laurie Drabble
Karen Trocki

SUMMARY. Relationships between sexual orientation and a wide range of substance use and problem variables were examined based on data from the 2000 National Alcohol Survey. Lesbians, bisexuals, and heterosexually identified women who report same-sex partners were compared to exclusively heterosexual women in relation to alcohol consumption, use of tobacco and other drugs, bar-going, alcohol-related

---

Laurie Drabble, PhD, is Assistant Professor at San Jose State University College of Social Work and an affiliate associate scientist with the Alcohol Research Group. Karen Trocki, PhD, is a scientist with the Alcohol Research Group, Berkeley, CA.

Address correspondence to: Laurie Drabble, San Jose State University College of Social Work, One Washington Square, San Jose, CA 95192-0124 (E-mail: ldrabble@sjsu.edu).

The authors would like to acknowledge Yu Ye and Jason Bond for their assistance with statistical analysis.

This research was supported by grants P50 AA05595 (National Alcohol Research Center) and R01 AA-08564 from the National Institute on Alcohol Abuse and Alcoholism.

[Haworth co-indexing entry note]: "Alcohol Consumption, Alcohol-Related Problems, and Other Substance Use Among Lesbian and Bisexual Women." Drabble, Laurie, and Karen Trocki. Co-published simultaneously in *Journal of Lesbian Studies* (Harrington Park Press, an imprint of The Haworth Press, Inc.) Vol. 9, No. 3, 2005, pp. 19-30; and: *Making Lesbians Visible in the Substance Use Field* (ed: Elizabeth Ettorre) Harrington Park Press, an imprint of The Haworth Press, Inc., 2005, pp. 19-30. Single or multiple copies of this article are available for a fee from The Haworth Document Delivery Service [1-800-HAWORTH, 9:00 a.m. - 5:00 p.m. (EST). E-mail address: docdelivery@haworthpress.com].

Available online at http://www.haworthpress.com/web/JLS
© 2005 by The Haworth Press, Inc. All rights reserved.
doi:10.1300/J155v09n03_03

problems, and past substance abuse treatment. Substance use patterns were complex and varied between sexual orientation groups. These differences underscore the importance of developing lesbian- and bisexual-sensitive prevention and treatment services and of including measures of sexual orientation identity and behavior in population-based surveys. *[Article copies available for a fee from The Haworth Document Delivery Service: 1-800-HAWORTH. E-mail address: <docdelivery@haworthpress.com> Website: <http://www.HaworthPress.com> © 2005 by The Haworth Press, Inc. All rights reserved.]*

KEYWORDS. Lesbians, bisexual women, sexual orientation, substance abuse, alcohol, tobacco, drugs, bar-going, drinking contexts

INTRODUCTION

Despite advances in research on lesbian health including alcohol, tobacco and other drug issues, only a few national population-based studies have included questions related to sexual orientation (Boehmer, 2002; Sell & Becker, 2001; Sell & Petrulio, 1996). A majority of studies related to lesbian health or substance use have relied on non-probability sampling methods and, consequently, are limited in generalizability to the larger population (Hughes & Eliason, 2002; Sell & Petrulio, 1996). Lesbian health advocates assert that innovative research designs that gather information about stigmatized and difficult to reach populations should not be devalued in comparison to quantitative studies based on random samples (Plumb, 2001). At the same time, researchers and advocates are calling for inclusion of questions related to different dimensions of sexual orientation in population-based surveys to facilitate examination of lesbian, gay, and bisexual health issues that may be generalizable to the larger population as is routinely available in relation to other demographic groups based on age, race/ethnicity, gender, and socioeconomic status (Sell & Becker, 2001; Sell & Petrulio, 1996; Solarz, 1999).

A few population-based surveys in recent years have contributed to an emerging understanding of substance use and abuse among lesbian and bisexual women. In general, these studies suggest that lesbians and bisexual women are less likely to abstain from alcohol, more likely to report heavier drinking, and more likely to report symptoms of alcohol dependence (Cochran, Keenan, Schober, & Mays, 2000; Cochran &

Mays, 2000; Diamant, Wold, Spritzer, & Gelberg, 2000; Gilman et al., 2001; Scheer et al., 2003; Valanis et al., 2000). Lesbians and bisexual women may also be more likely to have received treatment for alcohol-related problems (Cochran et al., 2000). One regional population-based study found no difference in alcohol use between self-identified lesbians and heterosexuals but found lesbians more likely to report being recovering alcoholics (Bloomfield, 1993). Lesbians and bisexual women may also be more likely to report tobacco use (Diamant et al., 2000; Valanis et al., 2000), drug use (Scheer et al., 2003), and drug dependence (Gilman et al., 2001). Although valuable, many of these studies have limitations. For example, national studies in the US have often used behavioral measures, such as sex of partners in a given time frame, to define sexual orientation and combined all women reporting same sex partners (Cochran et al., 2000; Cochran & Mays, 2000; Gilman et al., 2001). Consequently, these studies may fail to identify risks that may be associated with sexual orientation identity or that may differ between lesbians and bisexuals. Only a few population-based surveys on women's health disaggregated lesbians and bisexuals in analyses of health risk behaviors (Diamant et al., 2000; Scheer et al., 2003; Valanis et al., 2000); however, measures of alcohol consumption or other substance use were limited in these studies.

This national population-based study examines the relationship between sexual orientation and a wide range of substance use and problem variables including patterns of alcohol use, use of tobacco and other drugs, indicators of alcohol-related problems, past substance abuse treatment, and bar-going. In addition, the analysis described here disaggregates populations of women that are often combined, such as self-identified lesbians, self-identified bisexuals, and women who report same-sex partners yet identify as heterosexual.

Methods

The data used for this study are from the National Alcohol Survey conducted between November 1999 through June 2001. The Alcohol Research Group in Berkeley undertook a national household computer-assisted telephone interview (CATI) survey of the adult (18 or older) population in all 50 states of the US and Washington, D.C. (N = 7612). Interviews lasted 25 to 50 minutes. A Spanish language version was administered to Spanish speakers.

Measures

Sexual orientation was based on both a self-identity question and a sexual behavior question that asked respondents about the gender of sexual partners in the past five years. Using these measures, a four-category sexual orientation variable was created: lesbian identity, bisexual identity, heterosexual identity with reports of same sex-partners, and exclusively heterosexual (heterosexual identity with no reports of same-sex partners). Respondents who did not categorize themselves in response to the identity question (refused, did not know, or did not provide a response) were eliminated from this analysis (n = 262). Among women in the full sample, 96% (n = 3723) identified as heterosexual and reported exclusively opposite-sex partners in the past 5 years, 1.8% (n = 71) identified as heterosexual while reporting having had same-sex partners, 1.3% (n = 50) were bisexual, and 0.9% (n = 36 were lesbian).

Analysis

Respondents classified into the four sexual orientation categories were compared in relation to drinking status, drug use, tobacco use, negative social consequences, DSM-IV alcohol dependence, past treatment for alcohol or other drug problems, and bar patronage using chi-square tests. Tests for differences between groups were conducted using ANOVA, linear regression, and logistic regression. Five demographic variables were used as control variables in multivariate analyses: age, ethnicity, relationship status (partnered or not partnered), median income, and educational level.

Results

Patterns of Abstention, Drinking, and Heavier Drinking

Current drinker status was determined by an overall alcohol frequency question asked of all respondents and a more specific follow-up question that was asked of those respondents who drank infrequently, or who answered "don't know" or "refused" to determine if they drank any alcohol in the last year. In addition, two additional alcohol consumption measures were used in this analysis: (1) mean number of drinks in the last year based on a graduated frequency measure (Clark & Hilton, 1991) and (2) mean number of days drank five or more drinks also based on the graduated frequency measure (Greenfield, 2000).

Bivariate relationships were examined between sexual orientation and three categories of drinkers: non-drinkers, drinkers who did not engage in heavier drinking, and drinkers who had engaged in heavier drinking in the past year (defined as drinking five or more drinks on one or more occasions) (Drabble, Trocki, & Midanik, in press). Heterosexual women who reported exclusively opposite-sex partners had higher rates of abstention than other groups of women (although this difference did not reach significance in comparison to lesbians) and were significantly less likely to be heavier drinkers (12.7%) compared to bisexual women (45.6%, $p < .001$), lesbians (41.8%, $p < .001$) and heterosexual women who report same-sex partners (32.8%, $p < .001$). There was no difference in non-heavier drinking by sexual orientation.

The mean number of drinks per year was elevated among lesbians (336.4), bisexual women (466.4), and heterosexual women reporting same-sex partners (321.8) compared to exclusively heterosexual women (146.2). However, when controlling for demographic variables, only the difference between exclusively heterosexual women compared to women who identify as heterosexual and report same-sex partners was significant. Similarly, the mean number of days respondents reported drinking five or more drinks was somewhat higher among lesbians (25.2), bisexuals, (44.2), and heterosexual women reporting same-sex partners (18.8) compared to exclusively heterosexual women (7.2), although none of these differences were statistically significant when controlling for demographic variables.

Use of Tobacco and Illicit Drugs

Use of tobacco and illicit drugs was measured based on past year reports of any tobacco use, THC use (marijuana, hash, THC, or grass), or illicit drug use excluding marijuana (cocaine/crack, uppers, downers, hallucinogens, or heroin/opium). In the full sample of women, 26.6 percent ($n = 992$) reported tobacco use, 5.8 percent ($n = 220$) reported THC use, and approximately 6.1 percent ($n = 230$) reported other illicit drug use excluding THC. Compared to exclusively heterosexual women, the odds of past year tobacco use were over three times greater among bisexual women (Odds Ratio (OR) = 3.45, Confidence Interval (CI): 1.71-6.97, $p < .01$) and two times greater for heterosexually identified women who report same-sex partners (OR = 2.04, CI: 1.18-3.51, $p < .05$). Past year tobacco use was not significantly greater among lesbians. Even when controlling for other variables, odds of THC use were significantly greater among lesbians (OR = 4.70, CI: 1.58-13.99, $p <$

.01), bisexual women (OR = 6.09, CI: 3.10-11.95, p < .001), and heterosexually identified women who reported same-sex partners (OR = 3.94, CI: 1.89-8.16, p < .001) compared to exclusively heterosexual women. This difference was most pronounced among bisexual women. Use of illicit drugs (excluding THC) did not differ significantly by sexual orientation.

Alcohol-Related Problems, Alcohol Dependence, and Past Treatment

Respondents were classified as reporting alcohol-related problems if they reported two or more problems based on 15 items in five domains: legal/accidents, health, work, fights and relationship problems (Midanik & Clark, 1995). Respondents were considered positive for Diagnostic and Statistical Manual-Fourth Edition (DSM-IV) alcohol dependence if they reported three or more of the seven criteria in the last 12 months (Caetano, Tam, Greenfield, Cherpitel, & Midanik, 1997). Past treatment was defined based on an affirmative response to the following question: Did you ever receive treatment from a chemical dependency or substance abuse program for either alcohol or drugs? Among women drinkers, 3.2% (n = 70) reported two or more alcohol-related social consequences and 2.7% (n = 58) were positive for alcohol dependence. In the full sample, approximately 2.6% (n = 100) of women reported having received treatment for alcohol or other drugs.

Alcohol-related consequences and alcohol dependence among drinkers were examined in relation to sexual orientation (Drabble, Trocki, & Midanik, in press) and are depicted in Table 1. Past participation in any treatment for alcohol or drug problems reported among women in the full sample is also depicted in Table 1. There was no difference in any of these outcomes between the two categories of heterosexually identified women. By contrast, both lesbians and bisexual women had significantly greater odds of reporting current alcohol-related problems (negative consequences and alcohol dependence) compared to heterosexual women. The odds of reporting past treatment were approximately eight times greater among lesbians and over five times greater for bisexual women compared to heterosexual women with exclusively opposite-sex partners.

Follow-up analysis of the 15 items of the social consequences index found that six items were significantly associated with sexual orientation (Drabble, Trocki, & Midanik, in press). Lesbian and bisexual women were significantly more likely than heterosexual women to report experiencing the following alcohol-related problems: fights, argu-

TABLE 1. Odds of reporting social consequences, alcohol dependence (among drinkers), past treatment, frequency of time spent in bars (full sample), and drinks per bar-going occasion (among bar-going women).

	OR[a]	CI	P
Problem indicators			
2 or more social consequences (n = 2151)[1]			
Heterosexual identity/same sex partners	0.77	0.17, 3.59	
Bisexual	8.13	2.97, 22.23	<.001
Lesbian	10.94	3.19, 37.42	<.001
DSM-IV alcohol dependence (n = 2151)[1]			
Heterosexual identity/same sex partners	2.17	0.60, 7.85	
Bisexual	6.39	2.03, 20.05	<.01
Lesbian	7.06	1.81, 27.58	<.01
Past treatment (n = 3742)[1]			
Heterosexual identity/same sex partners	1.15	0.26, 5.02	
Bisexual	5.37	1.72, 16.75	<.01
Lesbian	7.84	2.57, 23.94	<.001
Bar patronage and bar drinking			
Bar patronage 1 + month (n = 3792)[1]			
Heterosexual identity/same sex partners	2.46	1.46, 4.14	<.01
Bisexual	1.43	0.72, 2.86	
Lesbian	2.47	1.18, 5.12	<.01
4 + drinks in bars (n = 961)[1]			
Heterosexual identity/same sex partners	3.46	1.62, 7.38	<.01
Bisexual	2.61	1.07, 6.34	<.01
Lesbian	1.58	0.46, 5.36	

Note: OR = odds ratios; CI = confidence intervals
[1] Reference Group, Heterosexual identity and no same sex partners
[a] Adjusted for age, race/ethnicity, relationship status and education

ments, a spouse being angry due to drinking, a physician suggesting reduction in drinking, lost time at work, and trouble with the law about drinking when driving was not involved. Additional comparative analyses were also conducted on follow-up questions asked of respondents who reported past treatment. Variables examined for this analysis included reasons for seeking treatment, problem type (alcohol, drugs or both) or program type (alcohol or drug) and satisfaction with treatment (very satisfied/mostly satisfied compared to indifferent/mildly dissatisfied/very dissatisfied). Only satisfaction with treatment was associated with sexual orientation. Although a majority of respondents were very satisfied or mostly satisfied with their experience in treatment, lesbians and bisexuals were significantly less likely to report feeling satisfied with the services they received than heterosexual women (58.3% compared to 86.3%, $p < .05$).

Bar-Going and Other Drinking Contexts

The odds of going to bars one or more times a month and the odds of drinking four or more drinks when drinking in bar contexts are depicted in Table 1. Heterosexually identified women who report same-sex partners are more likely both to go to bars and to drink heavily in bars. Lesbians are nearly 2.5 times more likely to go to bars than exclusively heterosexual women but are not more likely to drink heavily in bar settings. By contrast, bisexual women are not more likely to go to bars, but are more likely than exclusively heterosexual women to drink heavily in bars. Although few differences were found in attending parties once a month or more and drinking heavily in parties by sexual orientation categories (analysis not shown), bisexual women were approximately 3.5 times more likely to drink heavily in party contexts.

DISCUSSION

The findings of this study are, in general, consistent with the few population-based regional or national studies that found evidence for less abstention from alcohol and drugs among lesbians and bisexual women as well as greater indicators of substance abuse problems such as alcohol-related problems, alcohol dependence, or history of treatment among lesbians and bisexual women (Bloomfield, 1993; Cochran et al., 2000; Cochran & Mays, 2000; Diamant et al., 2000; Gilman et al., 2001; Scheer et al., 2003; Valanis et al., 2000). However, this study also suggests that some of these relationships between sexual orientation and substance use and abuse may be complex. For example, overall volume and number of days drinking five or more drinks among current drinkers did not appear to vary significantly among groups, with the exception of significantly greater mean number of drinks per year among heterosexual women who report same-sex partners in the past five years compared to heterosexual women who do not report same-sex partners. However, lesbians and bisexual women had vastly greater odds for reporting alcohol-related consequences and alcohol dependence. Since alcohol-related problems may occur at even fairly low levels of consumption (Midanik, Tam, Greenfield, & Caetano, 1996), indicators of heavier drinking and alcohol-related problems may be, in part, a function of less abstention and more social drinking.

Few studies have examined health behaviors among women who identify as heterosexual but report same-sex partners. In relation to some substance use behaviors, such as tobacco use and heavier drinking in bars, this population appears to have patterns that are similar to bisexual women. These same behaviors were not significantly greater among lesbians compared to heterosexual women. At the same time, both lesbian and bisexual identity appeared to be more salient in relation to risks for more serious alcohol-related problems such as alcohol-related consequences, dependence, or a history of receiving substance abuse treatment. Bisexual identity in particular appeared to be a fairly consistent predictor across many of the different substance abuse measures including heavier drinking in both bar and party contexts, other substance use such as tobacco and THC, and alcohol problem measures.

Some researchers have suggested that participation in drinking contexts such as bars may serve as a way to connect to social networks among lesbians and that drinking in these contexts is reflective of positive affiliation with community rather than pathological drinking (Heffernan, 1998; Parks, 1999). This is consistent with the finding that greater bar attendance among lesbians was not associated with heavier drinking in these contexts. Drinking as it may relate to developing social networks or to coping with stress of marginalization among bisexual women (defined by either identity or behavior) remains relatively unexplored. Although research to date is inconclusive, there is some evidence that bisexuals may feel marginalized in relationship to both heterosexual and lesbian communities (Fox, 1996).

In contrast to studies that found no difference in problem drinking but greater reports of past treatment among lesbians (Bloomfield, 1993; Hughes, Hass, Razzano, Cassidy, & Matthews, 2000), findings from this study suggest that both past treatment and problems among current drinkers are particularly high among lesbians and bisexual women. The greater likelihood of reporting history of treatment in our study is combined with the disturbing finding that lesbians and bisexual women are also less likely to report being satisfied with their treatment experience. This would appear to affirm the work of researchers and authors that have documented the need for both organizational and counselor level changes to create sensitive treatment services for lesbians and bisexual women (Barbara, 2002; Drabble & Underhill, 2002; Eliason, 2000).

It is not uncommon for researchers to rely on sexual behavioral measures as a proxy for sexual identity in national population-based research (Cochran et al., 2000; Cochran & Mays, 2000; Gilman et al., 2001; Valanis et al., 2000). Inclusion of behavioral measures of sexual orientation in population-based surveys is important. At the same time, the variations in risk between substance use and abuse outcomes between the sexual orientation categories of women in this study support arguments in favor of also including measures of identity in these surveys.

There are a number of limitations to this study. The number of respondents in any population-based survey that identify as lesbian or gay is inevitably small. Some of the differences between groups might have been significant if we had greater power to detect differences. Another limitation is that some respondents were not asked about their sexual behavior. All respondents were asked the sexual orientation identity question. However, respondents were not asked about past five year partners if they responded "none" to an earlier question, "In the last five years, how many people have you had sexual intercourse with?" It is possible that some respondents who do not associate the term intercourse with their own sexual practices were erroneously classified as not having had sex in the past 5 years.

In spite of these limitations, this study was based on a large, representative cross-section of the United States population. As such, it avoids some of the possible biases of purposive samples and regional population-based samples. It also demonstrates that both sexual orientation identity and sexual behavior questions can be successfully included in a national survey. Multiple measures of sexual orientation can, and should, be included in other national surveys related to alcohol and drugs, health and mental health. The results of this study also underscore the importance of developing substance abuse prevention and treatment interventions that are sensitive to lesbians and bisexual women.

REFERENCES

Barbara, A. (2002). Substance abuse treatment with lesbian, gay and bisexual people: A qualitative study of service providers. *Journal of Lesbian & Gay Social Services, 14*(4), 1-17.

Bloomfield, K. (1993). A comparison of alcohol consumption between lesbians and heterosexual women in an urban population. *Drug and Alcohol Dependence, 33*, 257-269.

Boehmer, U. (2002). Twenty years of public health research: Inclusion of lesbian, gay, bisexual, and transgender population. *American Journal of Public Health, 92*(7), 1125-1130.

Caetano, R., Tam, T., Greenfield, T. K., Cherpitel, C. J., & Midanik, L. T. (1997). DSM-IV alcohol dependence and drinking in the U.S. population: A risk analysis. *Annals of Epidemiology, 7*, 542-549.

Clark, W. B., & Hilton, M. E. (1991). *Alcohol in America: Drinking Practices and Problems*. Albany, NY: State University of New York Press.

Cochran, S. D., Keenan, C., Schober, C., & Mays, V. M. (2000). Estimates of alcohol use and clinical treatment needs among homosexually active men and women in the U.S. population. *Journal of Consulting and Clinical Psychology, 68*(6), 1062-1071.

Cochran, S. D., & Mays, V. M. (2000). Relation between psychiatric syndromes and behaviorally defined sexual orientation in a sample of the US population. *American Journal of Epidemiology, 151*(5), 516-523.

Diamant, A. L., Wold, C., Spritzer, K., & Gelberg, L. (2000). Health behaviors, health status and access to and use of health care: A population-based study of lesbian, bisexual, and heterosexual women. *Archives of Family Medicine, 9*, 1043-1051.

Drabble, L., Trocki, K. F., & Midanik, L. T. (in press). Reports of alcohol consumption and alcohol-related problems among homosexual, bisexual, and heterosexual respondents: Results from the 2000 National Alcohol Survey. *Journal of Studies on Alcohol*.

Drabble, L., & Underhill, B. L. (2002). Effective interventions and treatment for lesbians. In S. L. Straussner & S. E. Brown (Eds.), *Handbook for addiction treatment for women: Theory and practice* (pp. 399-422). New York: Jossey-Bass.

Eliason, M. J. (2000). Substance abuse counselors' attitudes regarding lesbian, gay, bisexual and transgender clients. *Journal of Substance Abuse, 12*, 311-328.

Fox, R. (1996). Bisexuality in perspective: A review of theory and research. In B. Firestein (Ed.), *Bisexuality: The psychology and politics of an invisible minority*. Thousand Oaks: Sage.

Gilman, S. E., Cochran, S. D., Mays, V. M., Hughes, M., Ostrow, D., & Kessler, R. C. (2001). Risk of psychiatric disorders among individuals reporting same-sex sexual partners in the National Comorbidity Survey. *American Journal of Public Health, 91*(6), 933-939.

Greenfield, T. K. (2000). Ways of measuring drinking patterns and the difference they make: Experience with graduated frequency. *Journal of Substance Abuse, 12*, 33-49.

Heffernan, K. (1998). The nature and predictors of substance abuse among lesbians. *Addictive Behaviors, 23*(4), 517-528.

Hughes, T. L., & Eliason, M. (2002). Substance use and abuse in lesbian, gay, bisexual and transgender populations. *Journal of Primary Prevention, 22*(3), 263-298.

Hughes, T. L., Hass, A. P., Razzano, L., Cassidy, R., & Matthews, A. (2000). Comparing lesbians' and heterosexual women's mental health: A multi-site survey. *Journal of Gay & Lesbian Social Services, 11*(1), 57-76.

Midanik, L. T., & Clark, W. B. (1995). Drinking-related problems in the United States: Descriptions and trends, 1984-1990. *Journal of Studies on Alcohol, 56*, 395-402.

Midanik, L. T., Tam, T. W., Greenfield, T. K., & Caetano, R. (1996). Risk functions for alcohol-related problems in a 1998 US national sample. *Addiction, 91*(10), 1427-1437.

Parks, C. (1999). Bicultural competence: A mediating factor affecting alcohol use practices and problems among lesbian social drinkers. *Journal of Drug Issues, 29*(1), 135-154.

Plumb, M. (2001). Undercounts and overstatements: Will the IOM report on lesbian health improve research. *American Journal of Public Health, 91*(6), 873-875.

Scheer, S., Parks, C. A., McFarland, W., Page-Shafer, K., Delgado, V., Ruiz, J. D. et al. (2003). Self-reported sexual identity, sexual behaviors and health risks: Examples from a population-based survey of young women. *Journal of Lesbian Studies, 7*(1), 69-83.

Sell, R. L., & Becker, J. B. (2001). Sexual orientation data collection and progress toward Healthy People 2010. *American Journal of Public Health, 91*(6), 876-882.

Sell, R. L., & Petrulio, C. (1996). Sampling homosexuals, bisexuals, gays and lesbians for public health research: A review of the literature from 1990 to 1992. *Journal of Homosexuality, 30*(4), 31-47.

Solarz, A. L. (Ed.). (1999). *Lesbian health: Current assessment and directions for the future. Institute of Medicine Committee on Lesbian Health Research Priorities.* Washington, D.C.: National Academy Press.

Valanis, B. G., Bowen, D. J., Bassford, T., Whitlock, E., Charney, P., & Carter, R. A. (2000). Sexual orientation and health. *Archives of Family Medicine, 9*, 843-853.

Alcohol Use and Alcohol-Related Problems in Self-Identified Lesbians: An Historical Cohort Analysis

Cheryl A. Parks
Tonda L. Hughes

SUMMARY. Age cohort and racial/ethnic differences in alcohol-use patterns and alcohol-related problems were examined in a diverse sample of self-identified lesbians using data from the Chicago Health and Life Experiences of Women Study (CHLEW). Significant differences in lifetime drinking patterns and lifetime alcohol-related problems were found across three generational cohorts; few differences were found across racial/ethnic groups. Findings are discussed in relation to previous research on lesbian alcohol use. *[Article copies available for a fee from The Haworth Document Delivery Service: 1-800-HAWORTH. E-mail address: <docdelivery@haworthpress.com> Website: <http://www.HaworthPress.com> © 2005 by The Haworth Press, Inc. All rights reserved.]*

Cheryl A. Parks, PhD, MSW, is Associate Professor at the School of Social Work, University of Connecticut. Tonda L. Hughes, PhD, RN, FAAN, is Associate Professor, College of Nursing, University of Illinois at Chicago.

Address correspondence to: Cheryl A. Parks, School of Social Work, University of Connecticut, W. Hartford, CT 06117-2698 (E-mail: cheryl.parks@uconn.edu).

The development of this paper was supported by grants from the National Institute of Alcohol Abuse and Alcoholism (NIAAA) # AA0026, AA13328 and AA014375.

[Haworth co-indexing entry note]: "Alcohol Use and Alcohol-Related Problems in Self-Identified Lesbians: An Historical Cohort Analysis." Parks, Cheryl A., and Tonda L. Hughes. Co-published simultaneously in *Journal of Lesbian Studies* (Harrington Park Press, an imprint of The Haworth Press, Inc.) Vol. 9, No. 3, 2005, pp. 31-44; and: *Making Lesbians Visible in the Substance Use Field* (ed: Elizabeth Ettorre) Harrington Park Press, an imprint of The Haworth Press, Inc., 2005, pp. 31-44. Single or multiple copies of this article are available for a fee from The Haworth Document Delivery Service [1-800-HAWORTH, 9:00 a.m. - 5:00 p.m. (EST). E-mail address: docdelivery@haworthpress.com].

Available online at http://www.haworthpress.com/web/JLS
© 2005 by The Haworth Press, Inc. All rights reserved.
doi:10.1300/J155v09n03_04

KEYWORDS. Lesbian, alcohol use, alcohol problems, race/ethnicity, cohorts

INTRODUCTION

Since the mid-1970s research on lesbians' alcohol use has sought to describe differences between lesbians' and heterosexual women's patterns of drinking. Investigators of two of the earliest studies reported rates of heavy or dependent drinking among lesbians that were more than three times as high as those of women in the general population (Fifield, Latham, & Phillips, 1977; Saghir & Robins, 1973). More recent research, using less biased samples, has found overall lower rates of heavy drinking among lesbians. Yet, differences in lesbians' and heterosexual women's drinking patterns and rates of drinking-related problems continue to be identified. Results of studies conducted in the 1980s and 1990s suggest that lesbians are less likely than heterosexual women to abstain from drinking or to reduce their alcohol use with age. Lesbians tend to report more indicators of alcohol-related problems than heterosexual women, even at comparable levels of consumption (see Hughes & Eliason, 2002 for detailed discussion; see also Diamant, Wold, Spritzer, & Gelberg, 2000; Gruskin, Hart, Gordon, & Ackerson, 2001; Jaffe, Clance, Nichols, & Emshoff, 2000; Valanis et al., 2000).

In general, comparisons between lesbians' and heterosexual women's drinking emphasize lesbians' greater risk for problem drinking. However, these studies usually treat lesbians as a homogeneous group. Relatively little attention has been given to comparisons between subgroups of lesbians. In part, this is because most studies of lesbians' use of alcohol have not included large enough samples of racial/ethnic minority lesbians to permit reliable analyses of within-group differences. Furthermore, few researchers have examined age differences in drinking patterns and problems among lesbians.

Race/ethnicity, age and, by extension, historical context likely have important influences on the alcohol-use patterns of lesbians. In part, this conclusion is based on results of national and population-based studies of alcohol use and alcohol-related problems in the U.S. that have demonstrated a link between these characteristics and women's drinking behavior. For example, social norms related to drinking are generally more restrictive for women than men, and for women of color compared with white women (Caetano & Clark, 1998; Collins & McNair, 2002). Rates of heavy drinking and drinking-related problems tend to be highest among young adults and to decrease with age, although age-related risks also vary by race/ethnicity (USDHHS, 2000). In contrast and attributed, in part, to the historical significance of gay bars (Hall, 1993), cultural norms regarding women's alcohol use have been more permissive in lesbian communities. Although racial/ethnic comparisons among lesbians are notably absent in the literature, studies of gay and bisexual men suggest that the drinking patterns of sexual minority men and women of color may be more like those of their sexual minority counterparts than of demographically comparable heterosexual women and men (Hughes & Eliason, 2002). Finally, just as the social acceptability and patterns of drinking among women have varied in different historical periods (Wilsnack, Wilsnack & Hiller-Sturmhoefel, 1994), the visibility and societal acceptance of lesbians and gay men have undergone substantial changes within the last half-century (Miller, 1995). The intersection of these changes has created different opportunities and constraints related to drinking (D'Augelli, Grossman, Hershberger, & O' Connell, 2001; Parks, 1999) and may confer more or less risk (or protection) to different age cohorts of lesbians.

To examine potential age cohort and racial/ethnic differences in lesbians' drinking, we analyzed data from the first phase of the Chicago Health and Life Experiences of Women (CHLEW) study. The CHLEW is a longitudinal study of a large and diverse sample of lesbians from the Chicago metropolitan area. We expected to find fewer age differences in rates of drinking and drinking-related problems within the CHLEW sample than reported among women in general population studies. Given the limited research on lesbians of color, our examination of race/ethnic differences in drinking patterns and drinking-related problems was more exploratory.

METHODS

Participants

Data were collected in 2000 and 2001. Women who lived in Chicago, were 18 years or older, and who identified as lesbian were recruited using a broad range of sources (lesbian/gay bars were excluded). In contrast to most research on lesbian health that includes relatively few women of color, only one-half of our sample is white. More detailed information about the sample and the study is reported in Bostwick and Hughes (this publication).

Instrument and Measures

Women were interviewed in person using a slightly modified version of the National Study of Health and Life Experiences of Women (NSHLEW) instrument and interview protocol. The NSHLEW is a 20-year study of women's drinking conducted by Sharon and Richard Wilsnack at the University of North Dakota (see, e.g., Wilsnack, Wilsnack, Kristjanson, & Harris, 1998). The 80-page CHLEW instrument contains over 400 items, permitting assessment of the individual and combined effects of a large number of risk and protective factors identified in previous theory and research as being associated with women's drinking. This paper focuses on a select few of these variables.

Racial/Ethnic Identity. Study participants were asked to choose which of seven racial groups–White, Black/African American, Asian or Pacific Islander, American Indian, Eskimo, Aleut, or other–most closely described their race. All respondents were then asked whether they were of Hispanic or Latino origin or descent. For purposes of this analysis, White (n = 210) and Black (n = 129) respondents were grouped according to the racial identity selected. Women who chose the "other" racial category and reported that they were of Hispanic or Latino origin or descent were categorized as Hispanic (n = 81). Twenty-seven respondents (6%) identified as Asian/Pacific Islander, Native American, or as bi- or multi-racial. Given their diversity and the small number of women in these racial/ethnic subgroups, they were excluded from the analyses.

Age Cohorts. Year of birth was used to assign respondents to one of three generational cohorts. Cohort assignments correspond to the timing of specific events in United States history that are considered significant to changes in the visibility and acceptance of lesbians and gay men in the U.S. (Parks, 1999). Respondents born before 1952 (ages 49 to 84 years) were included in the Stonewall (n = 85) cohort, those born in 1952 through 1967 (ages 33 to 48 years) in the Liberation (n = 183) cohort, and those born in 1968 or later (ages 18 to 32 years) were included in the Rights (n = 152) cohort.

Drinking Levels. The CHLEW contains multiple measures of drinking, including 30-day, 12-month, and lifetime drinking, derived from commonly used quantity and frequency questions. To calculate *current (30-day) drinking levels*, respondents indicated how often they had drunk wine, beer and liquor in the 30 days prior to their interview, and how many drinks of each alcoholic beverage they usually had on a day that they drank that beverage. Based on these quantity and frequency measures and the ethanol content for all three beverages, we calculated average daily ethanol consumption. Respondents were then classified as heavy (one or more ounces of ethanol per day), moderate (0.22 to 0.99 ounces/day), or light (< 0.22 ounces per day) drinkers. To determine *12-month drinking levels*, respondents indicated how frequently, on a monthly basis, they drank any alcoholic beverages and the number of drinks consumed on a typical day when they drank. Heavy drinking was defined as having two or more drinks daily or four or more drinks per occasion at any frequency. Moderate drinkers reported frequent (several times per week), low quantity drinking (1-3 drinks) or consumption of one drink daily. Women who reported infrequent (several times per month or less), low quantity drinking were classified as light drinkers. Standard quantity and frequency categories were used to assess *initial drinking level* and changes in drinking patterns. Levels of drinking included: light (1-3 drinks < once per week); moderate (1 drink on 4 or more days a week or 2-3 drinks on 1-3 days per week); and heavy (2 or more drinks > 3 days per week, or 4 or more drinks at any frequency). Women who stopped drinking, drank on only one occasion, or who never drank were classified as "abstinent." Age of *first heavy drinking* corresponded to the age of the first calculated heavy drinking level.

Drinking-Related Problems. Several measures from the HLEW were used to assess drinking-related problems experienced in the respondents' lifetimes and in the previous 12 months. Eight questions asked about *adverse drinking consequences* such as driving while drunk or high from alcohol or drinking-related harm to work or job chances (range 0-8). Symptoms of potential *alcohol dependence* included items such as memory lapses while drinking (blackouts), and morning drinking (range 0-5). Four *lifetime problem drinking indicators* included a global measure of concern about drinking ("*Have you ever wondered at any time if you were developing a drinking problem?*"), questions about whether respondents had ever been treated for alcohol-related problems and whether they were in recovery at the time of the interview, and a measure of any lifetime heavy drinking. Potential values on the problem-drinking index ranged from 0-4.

Data Analysis

Univariate statistics were used to describe initial, 12-month and 30-day drinking levels, lifetime and 12-month alcohol consequences and dependence symptoms, and lifetime problem drinking indicators for each age cohort and race/ethnic group. Differences across age cohorts and across race/ethnic groups were assessed using the General Linear Model (GLM) Univariate procedure. Post hoc evaluations to determine which of the groups differed from the others, taking into consideration different group sizes and unequal variances between groups, were conducted. Interaction effects of age cohort and race/ethnicity were also tested.

RESULTS

Study Sample

The sample included in these analyses (n = 420) is diverse in terms of age (M = 38.5 years; range 18-84) and racial/ethnic composition (50% White, 31% Black, 19% Hispanic). More than one-half (55%) of respondents have a bachelor's or graduate degree. About 26% of the sample had annual household incomes under $20,000 while 22% had incomes of $75,000 or more per year. Approximately two-thirds (67%) of respondents were in a committed relationship with a female partner and about one-fifth (21%) had children living with them at the time of the interview. Table 1 provides descriptive information for the three racial/ethnic groups.

Drinking Levels

Table 2 summarizes drinking levels and patterns by age cohort and by race/ethnic group. Only about 4% (15) of respondents were lifetime abstainers. The youngest (Rights) and middle (Liberation) cohorts were slightly more likely to report lifetime abstinence (4.0% and 3.8% respectively) than was the Stonewall cohort (2.4%), but differences were not statistically significant. Black respondents were slightly more likely (5.5%) than White (2.9%) or Hispanic (2.5%) respondents to be lifetime abstainers (p = .372). Among lifetime drinkers, age cohorts differed on initial, 12-month and 30-day drinking levels, age of drinking onset, and age of first heavy drinking. Age of first heavy drinking, initial, and 30-day heavy drinking differed by race.

Significant interaction effects of cohort and race on age of drinking onset ($p < .02$), age of initial heavy drinking ($p < .01$) and 12-month heavy drinking ($p < .05$) were found (data not presented), indicating that

TABLE 1. Demographic Characteristics (by Race/Ethnicity)

	White (n = 210)	Black (n = 129)	Hispanic (n = 81)	Total (n = 420)	P value
Current Age: Mean (s.d.)	41.2 (13.3)	36.2 (9.4)	35.1 (8.2)	38.5 (11.7)	a, b
	N (%)	N (%)	N (%)		P value
Education					
≤ High school	16 (7.6)	29 (22.5)	14 (17.3)	59 (14.0)	
Some college	43 (20.5)	54 (41.9)	32 (39.5)	129 (30.7)	a, b
Bachelor's degree	64 (30.5)	27 (20.9)	16 (19.8)	107 (25.5)	
Graduate	87 (41.4)	19 (14.7)	19 (23.5)	125 (29.8)	
Annual Household Income					
under $20,000	43 (20.5)	47 (36.4)	18 (22.2)	108 (25.7)	
$20,000-39,999	43 (20.5)	35 (27.1)	25 (30.9)	103 (24.5)	a
$40,000-74,999	61 (29.0)	31 (24.0)	25 (30.9)	117 (27.9)	
$75,000 +	63 (30.0)	16 (12.4)	13 (16.0)	92 (21.9)	
Cohort					
Stonewall	68 (32.4)	15 (11.6)	2 (2.5)	85 (20.2)	
Liberation	69 (32.9)	68 (52.7)	46 (56.8)	183 (43.6)	b
Rights	73 (34.8)	46 (35.7)	33 (40.7)	152 (36.2)	
Currently living with/in committed relationship	152 (72.4)	78 (60.5)	53 (65.4)	283 (67.4)	ns
Any Children					
Currently in household	30 (14.8)	36 (28.3)	21 (26.6)	87 (21.3)	ns
Ever	49 (23.3)	60 (46.5)	27 (33.3)	136 (32.4)	a

[a] White and Black respondents differ at $p \leq .001$
[b] White and Hispanic respondents differ at $p \leq .001$
[c] Black and Hispanic respondents differ at $p \leq .001$

the relationship between age and drinking differed for the three racial/ethnic groups. Before controlling for race, Stonewall respondents were significantly older than Liberation and Rights respondents when they began to drink and first drank heavily; both Stonewall and Liberation respondents were less likely than Rights respondents to report heavy drinking in the previous 12 months. After controlling for race, no cohort differences in ages of drinking onset or first heavy drinking were found among Black lesbians. Among white and Hispanic lesbians, earlier drinking onset and first heavy drinking were positively associated with younger age. Further, in contrast to White and Hispanic *Rights* respondents, reports of heavy drinking in the previous 12 months were highest among Black *Stonewall* respondents.

TABLE 2. Current and Lifetime Alcohol Use by Age Cohort and Race/Ethnicity (n = 420)

	Lifetime Abstainers N (%)	Age 1st Began to Drink 0 (sd)	Initial Heavy Drinker N (%)	Past 12 Month Abstainer N (%)	Past 12 Month Heavy Drinker N (%)	Past 30-Day Abstainer N (%)	Past 30-Day Heavy Drinker N (%)	Age 1st Heavy Drinking 0 (sd)
RACE/ETHNICITY								
Black	7 (6)	17.0 (3.7)	19 (16)	17 (14)	23 (19)	32 (26)	19 (16)	20.8 (5.6)
Hispanic	2 (3)	16.3 (4.6)	25 (32)	6 (8)	16 (20)	13 (17)	5 (6)	18.3 (4.1)
White	6 (3)	16.8 (4.2)	44 (22)	27 (13)	20 (10)	43 (21)	8 (4)	18.1 (4.6)
P value	ns	ns	c	ns	ns	ns	a	a, c
COHORTS								
Stonewall	2 (2)	18.6 (5.2)	9 (11)	12 (15)	8 (10)	19 (23)	7 (8)	22.3 (5.6)
Liberation	7 (4)	16.5 (4.0)	47 (27)	30 (17)	15 (9)	47 (26)	9 (5)	19.1 (5.4)
Rights	6 (4)	16.0 (3.2)	32 (22)	8 (6)	36 (25)	22 (15)	16 (11)	17.5 (3.2)
P value	ns	d, e	d	f	e, f	f	ns	d, e
TOTAL	15 (4)	16.7 (4.1)	88 (22)	50 (12)	59 (15)	88 (22)	32 (8)	18.9 (4.9)

[a] White and Black respondents differ at $p \leq .05$
[b] White and Hispanic respondents differ at $p \leq .05$
[c] Black and Hispanic respondents differ at $p \leq .05$
[d] Stonewall and Liberation respondents differ $p < .05$
[e] Stonewall and Rights respondents differ $p < .05$
[f] Liberation and Rights respondents differ $p < .05$

Drinking-Related Problems

Data for drinking-related problems are summarized in Table 3. Reports of lifetime adverse drinking consequences (range 0-8; M = 1.5) and alcohol dependence symptoms (range 0-5; M = 1.4) were moderately low for the sample as a whole. Differences by age cohort, but not by race/ethnicity, were found; Rights and Liberation respondents reported more adverse drinking consequences and dependence symptoms than Stonewall respondents. Findings were similar for 12-month drinking-related problems. Stonewall respondents reported fewer adverse drinking consequences than Liberation or Rights respondents. Women in the Rights cohort reported significantly more dependence symptoms than either the middle or oldest groups. Interaction effects by race and cohort were not significant.

TABLE 3. Drinking-Related Problems/Problem-Drinking Indicators by Age Cohort and Race/Ethnicity (Excluding Lifetime Abstainers)

	# Lifetime Negative Consequences (0-8) 0 (sd)	# Lifetime Dependency Symptoms (0-5) 0 (sd)	# 12-Month Negative Consequences (0-8) 0 (sd)	# 12-Month Dependency Symptoms (0-5) 0 (sd)	Problem Indicator Index (0-4) 0 (sd)	Any Lifetime Heavy Drinking? N (%)	Ever Wondered About an Alcohol Problem? N (%)	Ever Sought Help for a Drinking Problem? N (%)	Currently in Recovery? N (%)
RACE/ETHNICITY									
Black	1.4 (1.7)	1.4 (1.5)	.57 (1.1)	.62 (1.1)	1.2 (1.2)	59 (49)	41 (34)	27 (23)	12 (10)
Hispanic	1.8 (1.6)	1.6 (1.6)	.49 (.96)	.48 (.97)	1.2 (1.1)	46 (58)	32 (41)	11 (14)	5 (6)
White	1.5 (1.5)	1.4 (1.4)	.29 (.72)	.35 (.83)	1.2 (1.2)	104 (51)	96 (48)	34 (17)	14 (7)
P value	ns	ns	ns	ns	ns	ns	ns	ns	ns
COHORTS									
Stonewall	1.2 (1.3)	1.0 (1.2)	.17 (.54)	.20 (.75)	1.0 (1.2)	30 (36)	36 (44)	12 (15)	6 (7)
Liberation	1.8 (1.8)	1.5 (1.6)	.43 (1.0)	.37 (.91)	1.3 (1.2)	97 (55)	78 (45)	40 (23)	21 (12)
Rights	1.4 (1.5)	1.6 (1.4)	.53 (.94)	.70 (1.1)	1.1 (1.2)	82 (57)	55 (39)	20 (14)	4 (3)
P value	d	d, e	d, e	e, f	ns	d, e	ns	ns	f
TOTAL	1.5 (1.6)	1.4 (1.5)	.41 (.91)	.45 (.96)	1.2 (1.2)	209 (52)	169 (42)	72 (18)	31 (8)

[a] White and Black respondents differ at $p \leq .05$
[b] White and Hispanic respondents differ at $p \leq .05$
[c] Black and Hispanic respondents differ at $p \leq .05$
[d] Stonewall and Liberation respondents differ $p < .05$
[e] Stonewall and Rights respondents differ $p < .05$
[f] Liberation and Rights respondents differ $p < .05$

More than one-half (52%) of the sample reported lifetime heavy drinking and 42% indicated that they had wondered at some point whether they might be developing a drinking problem. Nearly one-fifth (18%) had sought help for a drinking-related problem and 8% were in recovery. The number of drinking problem indicators did not differ by age or race/ethnicity; however, the interaction effect of race and age on problem indicators was significant ($p < .05$; data not presented). Black Rights lesbians reported fewer problem indicators than the Black Liberation or Black Stonewall cohorts; White Stonewall lesbians reported fewer indicators than White lesbians in either the Liberation or Rights cohorts. No differences were found between Hispanic lesbians in the Liberation and Rights cohorts (the Hispanic Stonewall cohort was too small to permit reliable comparisons).

Discussion

Compared with general population norms, we found fewer lifetime abstainers and, among lifetime drinkers, fewer age differences in drinking levels and drinking-related problems in this sample of self-identified lesbians. In contrast to our finding that only 4% of study respondents were lifetime abstainers, general population studies typically find that 45%-50% of adult women report that they never drank alcohol (Grant, 1997; Wilsnack et al., 1994). Researchers have also found that younger women (18-34 years old) are more likely than older women to drink, to drink heavily, and to report alcohol-related problems, and rates of drinking and drinking-related problems tend to decrease with age (Grant, 1997; USDHHS, 2000; Wilsnack et al., 1994). Consistent with general population trends, the youngest (Rights) cohort in our sample (ages 18-32) was most likely to report current (30-day) and 12-month drinking. They were also most likely to report current heavy drinking (though differences were not statistically significant) and more than twice as likely as the Liberation (ages 33-48) and Stonewall (ages 49-84) cohorts to report heavy drinking in the past year. Compared with the younger and middle cohorts, Stonewall respondents were older when they first began to drink and when they first drank heavily and were least likely to report initial or lifetime heavy drinking. They also reported the fewest lifetime and 12-month alcohol-related consequences and dependence symptoms.

In contrast, drinking levels and drinking-related problems among lesbians in the Liberation cohort were less consistent with general population norms. As expected, Liberation lesbians began drinking and reported first heavy drinking at ages younger than Stonewall and older than Rights respondents. Yet, they were more likely than both the older and the younger cohorts to report initial heavy drinking. Although differences were not significant, a trend toward greater abstinence and less heavy drinking among Liberation compared to Stonewall lesbians was observed. This trend may reflect a greater proportion of Liberation lesbians in alcoholism recovery. That is, higher rates of abstinence in this group may be a response to higher rates of lifetime heavy drinking and drinking related problems.

Considered together, these findings provide limited support for the hypothesis that the "maturing out" trend among lesbians is less evident than in heterosexual samples. Findings raise questions about earlier investigators' interpretations of age-related drinking patterns among lesbians. Because studies of lesbians' drinking (like most studies of lesbian health) typically include samples that are relatively young (25-45 years old), the absence of age-related declines in drinking rates and drinking-related problems found in previous studies may be a function of the restricted age range of the study samples. For example, Grant (1997) reports substantial increases in 12-month abstinence rates among women after age 45 and again after age 55 among respondents to the 1992 National Longitudinal Alcohol Epidemiologic Survey (NLAES). Most of the differences in our study were in comparisons of lesbians 49 years old or older with the two younger (18-32 and 33-48 years) cohorts; we found relatively few differences between the youngest and middle cohorts. Also important to consider in comparing our findings with those of other studies are the time frames assessed. In two previous studies addressing age-related patterns of drinking among lesbians, Bradford, Ryan, and Rothblum (1994) and McKirnan and Peterson (1989) assessed only current or past year alcohol use and alcohol-related problems. Our findings related to current (30-day) and 12-month drinking are consistent with findings reported in these studies. However, unlike these earlier investigators, we also assessed lifetime drinking and found significant differences between the oldest (Stonewall) and the middle (Liberation) cohort in age of drinking onset, age of first heavy drinking, number of lifetime drinking-related problems and likelihood of lifetime heavy drinking. Thus, focusing on more recent drinking outcomes provides only a limited picture of lesbians' drinking patterns and problems.

General population studies comparing alcohol use and alcohol-related problems among Black, Hispanic and White women find that White women are least likely to abstain from drinking, Black women are most likely to abstain, and rates of abstention for Hispanic women generally fall in between (Wilsnack et al., 1994). Further, although rates of frequent heavy drinking are generally low in all three racial/ethnic groups (range 2%-5%), Black women tend to report higher rates than White or Hispanic women (Caetano & Clark, 1998). We found few differences in levels of alcohol use or drinking-related problems across race/ethnic groups in our sample. Black lesbians first reported heavy drinking at significantly later ages than either White or Hispanic lesbians, but they were more likely than White lesbians to report current heavy drinking, and less likely than Hispanic lesbians to report initial heavy drinking. There were no differences across groups in lifetime, past 12-month or current rates of abstinence or in the number of lifetime or 12-month alcohol-related problems. Patterns related to age of drinking onset, age of first heavy drinking, and 12-month heavy drinking did differ by race across age cohorts, suggesting a potentially heightened risk for alcohol-related problems among older Black and younger White and Hispanic lesbians.

Limitations

Several important limitations should be considered in interpretation of this study's findings. The study used non-probability sampling methods and was restricted geographically to the Chicago metropolitan area. Although the diversity of the sample suggests that it is more representative of lesbians than many earlier studies, we cannot evaluate how well our sample represents lesbians as a whole or, in particular, lesbians of color or non-urban lesbians. At best, women in the CHLEW represent lesbians who are "out" enough to participate in an in-person interview about lesbian health. The size and diversity of the CHLEW sample provided adequate statistical power for the bivariate analyses reported yet the small numbers of older Black and Hispanic respondents limited our analyses of cohort by race interaction effects. Finally, all data were collected using self-report measures that are subject to recall bias. Potential differences in recall bias across cohorts should be considered when interpreting inter-cohort comparisons.

In summary, we found overall lower rates of current heavy drinking and drinking-related problems than reported in previous studies of lesbians' alcohol use. Nevertheless, the high rates of lifetime and current drinking, as well as the high rates of lifetime heavy drinking and other problem-drinking indicators (e.g., concern about drinking, treatment for alcohol-related problems) support the designation of lesbians as a population "at risk" for alcohol-related health problems.

REFERENCES

Bostwick, W., Hughes, T.L., & Johnson, T. (2005). The co-occurrence of depression and alcohol dependence symptoms in a community sample of lesbians. *Journal of Lesbian Studies, 9*(3), 7-18.

Bradford, J., Ryan, C., & Rothblum, E. D. (1994). National Lesbian Health Care Survey: Implications for mental health care. *Journal of Consulting & Clinical Psychology, 62*(2), 228-242.

Caetano, R., & Clark, C. L. (1998). Trends in alcohol consumption patterns among Whites, Blacks and Hispanics: 1984-1995. *Journal of Studies on Alcohol, 59*, 659-668.

Collins, R.L. & McNair, L.D. (2002). Minority women and alcohol use. *Alcohol Research & Health, 26* (4), 215-256.

D'Augelli, A. R., Grossman, A. H., Hershberger, S. L., & O' Connell, T. S. (2001). Aspects of mental health among older lesbian, gay, & bisexual adults. *Aging & Mental Health, 5(2)*, 149.

Diamant, A. L., Wold, C., Spritzer, K., & Gelberg, L. (2000). Health behaviors, health status, and access to and use of health care: A population-based study of lesbian, bisexual, and heterosexual women. *Archives of Family Medicine, 9*, 1043-1051.

Fifield, L. H., Latham, J. D., & Phillips, C. (1977). *Alcoholism in the gay community: The price of alienation, isolation and oppression (Unpub.)*. Los Angeles, CA: Gay Community Services Center.

Grant, B.F. (1997). Prevalence and correlates of alcohol use and DSM-IV alcohol dependence in US: Results of the National Longitudinal Alcohol Epidemiology Survey. *Journal of Studies on Alcohol, 58*, 464.

Gruskin, E. P., Hart, S., Gordon, N., & Ackerson, L. (2001). Patterns of cigarette smoking and alcohol use among lesbians and bisexual women enrolled in a large health maintenance organization. *American Journal of Public Health, 91*(6), 976-979.

Hall, J.M. (1993). Lesbians and alcohol: Patterns and paradoxes in medical notions and lesbian's beliefs. *Journal of Psychoactive Drugs, 25*(2), 109-119.

Hughes, T. L., & Eliason, M. (2002). Substance use and abuse in lesbian, gay, bisexual and transgender populations. *Journal of Primary Prevention, 22*(3), 263-298.

Jaffe, C., Clance, P. R., Nichols, M. F., & Emshoff, J. G. (2000). The prevalence of alcoholism and feelings of alienation in lesbian and heterosexual women. *Journal of Gay and Lesbian Psychotherapy, 3*(3/4), 25-35.

McKirnan, D. J., & Peterson, P. L. (1989). Alcohol and drug use among homosexual men and women: Epidemiology and population characteristics. *Addictive Behaviors, 14*(5), 545-553.

Miller, N. (1995). *Out of the past: Gay and lesbian history from 1869 to the present*. New York: Vintage.

Parks, C. A. (1999). Lesbian social drinking: The role of alcohol in growing up and living as lesbian. *Contemporary Drug Problems, 26*(1), 75-129.

Saghir, M. T., & Robins, E. (1973). *Male and female homosexuality: A comprehensive investigation*. Baltimore: Williams & Wilkins Co.

U.S. Department of Health and Human Services (USDHHS). (2000). *10th Special report to the U.S. Congress on alcohol and health (pp.28-53).* Washington DC: Author.

Valanis, B. G., Bowen, D. J., Bassford, T., Whitlock, E., Charney, P., & Carter, R. A. (2000). Sexual orientation and health. *Archives of Family Medicine, 9*(9), 843.

Wilsnack, S. C., Wilsnack, R. W., & Hiller-Sturmhoefel, S. (1994). How women drink: Epidemiology of women's drinking and problem drinking. *Alcohol Health & Research World, 18*(3), 173-181.

Wilsnack, R.W., Wilsnack, S.C., Kristjanson, A.F., & Harris, T.R. (1998). Ten-year prediction of women's drinking behavior in a nationally representative sample. *Women's Health: Research on Gender, Behavior and Policy, 4,* 199-230.

Substance Use and Social Identity in the Lesbian Community

Molly Kerby
Richard Wilson
Thomas Nicholson
John B. White

SUMMARY. Although the study results report discrepancies in the rates of substance abuse in the lesbian community, the general consensus in the field of gay and lesbian studies is that these individuals, as a whole, have a higher rate of substance use. For this study, data were collected via the Internet on the use of drugs and alcohol, level of self-esteem, and degree of social identity in the lesbian community. A correlation analysis was used to determine if negative social identity within the lesbian community leads to low self-esteem that is reflected in higher rates of substance abuse. Though a positive relationship between social identity and self-esteem was determined, no significant correlation between negative social identity, low self-esteem, and substance use was determined. How-

---

Molly Kerby, MPH, is a women's studies instructor at Western Kentucky University. Richard Wilson, PhD, is Professor of Public Health at Western Kentucky University. Thomas Nicholson, PhD, is Professor of Public Health at Western Kentucky University. John B. White, PhD, is Associate Professor of Public Health in the Department of Public Health, Western Kentucky University.

Address correspondence to: Molly Kerby, MPH, Women's Studies Instructor, Western Kentucky University, 1 Big Red Way, Women's Studies Center, Bowling Green, KY 42101 (E-mail: molly.kerby@wku.edu).

[Haworth co-indexing entry note]: "Substance Use and Social Identity in the Lesbian Community." Kerby, Molly et al. Co-published simultaneously in *Journal of Lesbian Studies* (Harrington Park Press, an imprint of The Haworth Press, Inc.) Vol. 9, No. 3, 2005, pp. 45-56; and: *Making Lesbians Visible in the Substance Use Field* (ed: Elizabeth Ettorre) Harrington Park Press, an imprint of The Haworth Press, Inc., 2005, pp. 45-56. Single or multiple copies of this article are available for a fee from The Haworth Document Delivery Service [1-800-HAWORTH, 9:00 a.m. - 5:00 p.m. (EST). E-mail address: docdelivery@haworthpress.com].

Available online at http://www.haworthpress.com/web/JLS
© 2005 by The Haworth Press, Inc. All rights reserved.
doi:10.1300/J155v09n03_05

ever, it is important to consider that respondents with *higher* levels of self-esteem reported more frequent use of specific drugs. That outcome in itself is an implication for further investigation. *[Article copies available for a fee from The Haworth Document Delivery Service: 1-800-HAWORTH. E-mail address: <docdelivery@haworthpress.com> Website: <http://www.HaworthPress.com> © 2005 by The Haworth Press, Inc. All rights reserved.]*

KEYWORDS. ATOD use, social identity, self-esteem, lesbian health, lesbian substance use

INTRODUCTION

While current research in the area of lesbian health problems is limited (Bernhard, 2001), it is evident that not only is access to health care restricted for lesbian and bisexual women but also homophobic attitudes still exist among health care professionals (Bernard, 2001; Cochran, 2004; Eliason, 2004). Substance abuse among women tends to be highly stigmatized in American culture and being both a lesbian and substance abuser dramatically increases that degree of stigmatization (Stern, 1993). Although there are reported discrepancies in the rates of substance abuse in the lesbian community, the general consensus is that some lesbians have high rates of substance use (Cochran, 2004), constitute part of a high-risk population (Bradford, Ryan, & Rothblum, 1994; Cochran, 2004; Eliason, 2004; Fortunata & Kohn, 2003; Gruskin, 2001; Heffernan, 1998; Hughes, 2003; Olmsted, 2004; Parks, 1999; Sorensen & Roberts 1997) and have higher rates of alcohol, tobacco and other drug use (ATOD) than heterosexual women. Some studies suggest that drinking patterns of lesbians are more consistent with national norms for male than female drinkers (Rosser, 1994). Obtaining accurate information on the prevalence of substance use and abuse in the gay and lesbian community is generally difficult because these populations are, for the most part, "hidden" from society (Stern, 1993).

Theoretical Considerations

In a widely used gay identity model, Cass (1990) describes sexual orientation development as a complex process with six stages of development including: (1) Identity Confusion; (2) Identity Comparison; (3) Identity

Tolerance; (4) Identity Acceptance; (5) Identity Pride; and (6) Identity Synthesis. Stages 1 through 3 describe the psychological processes involved in identity development from defining homosexual thoughts, emotions, and/or actions (e.g., *I may be gay*) to accepting these thoughts, emotions, and/or actions as homosexual (e.g., *I am gay*). Stages 4 through 6 describe the psychosocial aspects of identity development. These are the stages in which identity is defined through the individual's perception of social expectations ranging from fear of family and friends discovering one's sexual orientation to being an integrated part of the heterosexual society. The latter three stages are related to the development of *social identity*. At this point, individual identities are categorized by membership in the gay as well as heterosexual community.

Social identity theory was formulated by Henri Tajfel (1978) and is an important social psychological theory of intergroup relations and group processes. Central to social identity theory is the tenet that individuals are connected to social structures through self-definitions as members of certain social categories. While there is no implication of right or wrong ideologies within these social structures, there is a conception of the social structure that forms individual social identities as a member of particular social categories (Abrams & Hogg, 1990).

Social identity theory is based on two underlying processes: categorization and self-enhancement. Categorization is the cognitive process that assigns subjective meaning to stereotypes and norms in a group or category and allows for individual interpretation. Stereotypical perceptions of a particular group are an individual's image of certain sets of characteristics, either favorable or unfavorable, that define that entire group. Self-enhancement guides the social categorization process ensuring that these perceived norms and stereotypes are favorable (Robinson, 1996). In other words, it is assumed that an individual's membership in a particular group is a categorization of *positive* stereotypes and normative beliefs. However, both processes may differ depending on the status of the individual and her definition of acceptable behavior in specific situations.

METHODS

Aim of the Study

The aim of the study was to determine the existence of a relationship between negative social identity and low self-esteem, reflected in higher levels of substance abuse in the lesbian community. The investigators compared data among these three variables and determined how they relate to specific demographic information. A second aim was to explore the use of the Internet as a research method for accessing hard-to-reach populations.

Design and Procedure

The data collection method employed was a type of nonprobability sampling procedure referred to as a purposive sample. The survey instrument consisted of 44 questions arranged in four separate components: (1) factual questions designed to elicit demographic information; (2) subjective information designed to elicit respondents' perception of how well they "fit" in the heterosexual community; (3) behavioral information involving alcohol and drug use habits; and (4) subjective questions examining respondents' perception of their substance use. The research hypothesis was that negative social identity within the lesbian community leads to low self-esteem that is reflected in higher rates of substance abuse ($\alpha = .05$).

The first section of the survey contained the independent variables: sexual orientation, race, age, age of "coming out," relationship status, employment status, education, and religious preference. These variables represent demographic information that could have an effect on respondents' level of social identity as well as their alcohol and drug use behavior.

The second section was a series of subjective experience questions (i.e., subjective definition of reality) both positively and negatively worded, regarding social identity. These dependent variable items were based on a forced-answer, two-category set of responses, each item calling for one of the fixed-alternative expressions "T" (signifying true) or "F" (signifying false). For this response dichotomy, numerical weights of 0 and 1 were assigned to the positively worded questions. The order was reversed, 1 and 0, for the negatively worded questions. This method of reverse coding was used to assess internal validity. Scores above the intermediate values were identified as the "positive social identity category," and scores below were the "negative social identity category." The dependent variable of social identity was therefore dichotomous.

The third section was designed to measure alcohol and drug use patterns among the participants. These questions concerning ATOD use were taken from the National Household Drug Survey (United States

Department of Health and Human Services, 1996). Only questions involving the frequencies of use were utilized for this study.

The last questions involved respondents' perception of their behavior: (a) I do not have a problem with alcohol or drugs of any kind, (b) I am worried about my alcohol and/or drug use, (c) I am currently seeking help for my alcohol and/or drug problem, and (d) I should seek professional help for my alcohol and/or drug problem.

To reduce researcher bias and strengthen the validity of the study, a pilot study was conducted using a convenience sample (n = 50) of clientele from a fall retreat/workshop for lesbians at a bed and breakfast in northern Ohio. The survey process was completed through direct administration rather than on the Internet. Anonymized respondents were selected on voluntary bases and were also asked for suggestions on improving the questionnaire. Cronbach's alpha was used to measure the internal reliability of the multi-item indices and evaluate the validity and reliability of the questionnaire. As a result of this pilot study, several survey changes were made before administering it to the target population.

In order to effectively recruit respondents from the lesbian population, the survey was placed on a Web page and posted on the Internet. The site was hosted by a local Internet service provider, registered with all available search engines and indexed through five key words to aid visitors accessing the site. To solicit lesbian participation, the survey was linked to various lesbian organizations involved in Internet interactions such as the Lesbian Resource Project and National Lesbian Political Action Committee. The site was also incorporated into the Lesbian Health Web ring. Those who did not identify as lesbian were directed to exit the page. Respondents were self-selected and the size of the sample depended upon the number of willing respondents in the lesbian community, given that respondents were not invited to participate or contacted directly. A similar study using the Internet as a tool for collecting data on the prevalence of recreational illicit drug use is currently being conducted and is entitled DRUGNET (Nicholson, White, Cline, Minors, & Duncan, 2001).

The final instrument was written using Hyper Text Markup Language (HTML), and a Practical Extraction and Report Language (PERL) script for handling anonymous Common Gateway Interface (CGI) forms was used to process the survey responses. The files were stored in tab delimited text files that could be seamlessly pulled into an SPSS data file for analysis. The survey was placed on the Internet in August 2000, and data were collected until March 2001 using a URL provided by a local Internet Service Provider.

RESULTS

Usable data were collected from 76 respondents from the lesbian and bisexual female community and included in the final analysis. The majority of the respondents (77.6%) considered themselves to be lesbian, and 21.1% considered themselves to be bisexual. Over half (60%) of the respondents were between ages of 18-34 years, 82.7% were under the age of 45, and only 17% of the respondents reported that they were over the age of 45. The majority (93%) of the respondents had some education beyond high school, and 28% had graduated either from college or a post-secondary institution. Approximately 60% reported they were currently in some sort of a relationship with the remainder reporting that they were single (or not in a relationship). An overwhelming majority (81.1%) of the respondents were employed at least part-time and 60.8% were employed full-time. Only one person indicated that she was unemployed and 13 women reported some other employment status (Table 1).

The results of a correlation analysis indicated that there was a significant positive relationship between negative social identity and low self-esteem ($p < .0001$) among the respondents who completed the survey; a significant relationship between the use of marijuana and negative social identity ($p < .05$); and, a positive relationship between *higher* self-esteem and the use of excessive alcohol use ($p < .001$), amphetamines ($p < .001$), speed ($p < .001$), tranquilizers ($p < .01$), narcotics ($p < .01$), cocaine ($p < .01$), sedatives ($p < .01$), and inhalants ($p < .05$). Though the use of several specific drugs seemed to be related to self-esteem, social identity did not prove to be a significant factor in the relationship among the three constructs (Table 2).

A distribution describing the respondents' frequency of use of particular substances including use of alcohol, tobacco, sedatives, tranquilizers, narcotics, marijuana, inhalants, and cocaine is shown in Table 3. Forty percent of the respondents indicated that they consumed alcohol either daily or frequently, while 20% reported that they had *gotten very high or drunk* either daily or frequently. Almost half (47.2%) of the respondents reported that they smoked either daily or frequently.

TABLE 1. Demographics of Lesbian and Bisexual Females in the Study (n = 76)

Characteristics	n	%
Sexual Orientation		
Lesbian	59	77.6
Bisexual	16	21.1
*Neither	1	.01
Age		
18-24 years old	24	32.0
25-34 years old	21	28.0
35-44 years old	17	22.7
45-54 years old	7	9.3
55-64	5	6.7
65+	1	1.3
Highest Level of Education		
High school graduate/GED	5	6.7
Some college or post secondary school	28	37.3
College or post secondary graduate	21	28.0
Some graduate work	3	12.0
Graduate or professional degree	12	16.0
Relationship Status		
Single (no significant other)	31	40.8
Not co-habitating (but have significant other)	18	23.7
Co-habitating w/same sex partner	17	22.4
Other	10	13.2
Employment Status		
Full-time	45	60.8
Part-time	15	20.3
Unemployed	1	1.4
Other	13	17.6

Note. Respondents replying "Neither" were instructed to exit.

DISCUSSION

A correlation analysis was used to determine if negative social identity within the lesbian community leads to low self-esteem that is reflected in higher rates of substance abuse. Though a positive relationship between social identity and self-esteem was determined, no significant correlation between negative social identity, low self-esteem, and substance use was determined. However, it is important to consider that respondents with *higher* levels of self-esteem reported more frequent use of alcohol, tobacco, amphetamines, speed, sedatives,

TABLE 2. Correlation Matrix of Substance Use Behaviors of the Respondents (n = 76). *Regressed on Social Identity (SI) and Self-Esteem (SE) (Pearson Correlation - Sig. (one-tailed))

	SI	SE
SI	1.000	**.483 .000
SE	**.483 .000	1.000
Use of sedatives	.006 .481	*.242 .035
Use of tranquilizers	−.048 .362	*.242 .035
Use of amphetamines	.100 .230	*.325 .007
Use of inhalants	.127 .173	*.246 .032
Use of "coke"	**.601 .000	**343 .005

** Indicates p < .001. *Indicates p < .05.
Note: Table shows only significant variables.

TABLE 3. Respondents' Reported Percent of Use of Particular Substances (n = 76)

	Daily	Frequently	Several times a week	A few times in the last 12 months	Have not used in the last 12 months
How often consumed alcohol	10.9	27.9	18.6	29.5	13.1
Gotten very high or drunk	6.6	8.8	17.0	41.2	26.4
Used sedatives	2.7	2.2	2.2	7.7	85.2
Used tranquilizers	3.3	*--	3.7	8.2	84.6
Used amphetamines	2.2	3.3	1.6	17.0	75.8
Used narcotics	2.2	4.3	4.9	15.8	72.8
Used marijuana	5.6	5.6	7.2	17.8	63.9
Used inhalants	1.6	.5	.5	4.3	93.0
Used cocaine	2.7	*--	1.1	10.9	85.3
Smoked cigarettes	46.7	4.3	2.2	8.7	38.0

Note. Dashes indicate that percentages fell below .5%.

tranquilizers, barbiturates, cocaine, and inhalants because that outcome in itself is an implication for further investigation.

Though it is widely believed that low self-esteem is associated with greater substance use, research has not consistently supported this relationship and some research indicates that there is no correlation (Schroader & Laflin, 1993; Sullum, 1998). However, there is little conclusive research concerning specific behavior that deviates from societal norms using self-esteem as a construct in the predication of ATOD use. The findings in this study indicated that lesbians with higher self-esteem and a more positive social identity tend to use alcohol and drugs more frequently. One interpretation of this could be that individuals with higher self-esteem and a more positive social identity would be more likely to frequent *gay bars* and network in gay and lesbian culture.

Gay bars have traditionally provided a safe place for socialization for members of the lesbian community. These bars create an accepting community away from the prejudices of society. Unfortunately, they also promote the use of alcohol and other substances (Parks, 1999). Therefore, breaking away from the security of the bar may present threats of isolation to many lesbians that are not found in the heterosexual community. As a result, for those who are chemically dependent, recovery is not only the process of overcoming an addiction but a rebuilding of social networks as well. Severing codependent relationships is often necessary for all recovering addicts, even when their social networks are not a construct of shared sexual identity (Parks, 1999). Since most twelve-step recovery programs are constructed around the notion of empowerment, many lesbians oppose them because they feel that such programs are hypocritical in that they are a product of the white, male, Christian, middle-class culture that serve as the oppressor (Stern, 1993).

For these reasons, there is a pressing need for intervention and treatment programs that address the specific needs of the lesbian community. The issue ATOD use in the lesbian community is complex, and simply approaching only the issue of addiction is ineffectual. Programs designed for this community must incorporate the multiple causes of ATOD use and be tailored according to these unique characteristics.

Limitations

The outcome of this particular study may have been different if another sampling design was chosen. Using the Internet for data collection can be extremely time consuming because the researcher has no means of directly approaching respondents and success depends solely on that percentage of individuals who have access to the Internet.

Another important barrier was the unavailability of well-designed existing scales for measuring social identity. Since social identity is a concept based on individual perception, determining what constitutes negative and positive attributes is problematic. The study was also limited by subject matter. Though the concept is rapidly changing, the Internet has been consistently viewed as a source of entertainment not as a means for education and data collection.

The lack of correlation among social identity, self-esteem, and ATOD use may be a result of the small sample size (n = 76). According to Nachmias and Nachmias (1992), the size of the sample inherently produces the standard error; therefore, the smaller the sample, the higher the potential for error. Also, this sample was not a random one, drawing conclusions about the behaviors of lesbians in the general population is limited (Bohrnstedt & Knoke, 1994). A larger, random sample from the entire population would have provided greater opportunity for determining correlation among the variables, but when surveying hidden populations that is rarely an option.

Conclusions

The findings in this study should not deter continued research in this area but rather further interest in the relationship between gay and lesbian culture and alcohol and drug use. In addition, efforts should be made to develop scales that will more accurately measure social identity and self-esteem. It would also be interesting to explore the relationship discovered between high self-esteem and the use of sedative, tranquilizers, speed, and inhalants because these drugs, as well as others, have been associated with the bar culture.

Finally, using the Internet as a survey method has great implications for the future. It will provide an opportunity to reach those populations that would otherwise be unavailable for study. Though these data were collected for the purpose of this research project, the data collection is continuing in order to increase the sample size.

REFERENCES

Abrams, D. & Hogg, M. (Eds.). (1990). *Social identity theory: Constructive and critical analysis*. New York: Springer-Verlag.

Bernard, L. A. (2001). Lesbian health and health care. *Annual Review of Nursing Research, 19*, 145-177.

Bohrnstedt, G. & Knoke, D. (1994). *Statistics for social data analysis*. Illinois: F.E. Peacock.

Bradford, J., Ryan, C., & Rothblum, E. (1994). National lesbian health care survey: Implications for mental health care. *Journal of Consulting and Clinical Psychology, 62*, 228-242.

Cass, V. (1990). *Homosexuality/heterosexuality: Concepts of sexual orientation*. New York: Oxford University Press.

Cochran, B. (2004). Sexual minorities in substance abuse treatment: The impact of provider biases and treatment outcomes. *Dissertation Abstracts International, 64(8-B)*, 4027.

Eliason, M. (2004). Treatment counselor's attitudes about lesbian, gay, bisexual, and trangendered clients: Urban vs. rural settings. *Substance Use and Misuse, 39(40)*, 625-645.

Fortunata, B., & Kohn, C. S. (2003). Demographic, psychosocial, and personality characteristics of lesbian batterers. *Violence and Victims, 18*, 557-568.

Gruskin, E. P. (2001). Patterns of cigarette smoking and alcohol use among lesbians and bisexual women enrolled in a large health maintenance organization. *American Journal of Public Health, 91*, 976-980.

Heffernan, K. (1998). The nature and predictors of substance use among lesbians. *Addictive Behaviors, 23*, 517-528.

Hughes, T. L. (2003). Lesbians' drinking patterns: Beyond the data. *Substance Use and Misuse, 38*, 1739-1758.

Nachmias, C. & Nachmias, D. *Research Methods in the Social Sciences. (4th ed.)*. New York: St. Martin's Press.

Nicholson, T., White, J., Cline, R., Minors, P. & Duncan, D. (2001). Parents who report using illicit drugs: Findings and implications from the DRUGNET study. *Psychological Reports, 88*, 245-252.

Olmsted, T. (2004). To what extent are key services offered in treatment programs for special population? *Journal of Substance Abuse Treatment, 27(1)*, 9-15.

Parks, C. A. (1999). Bicultural competence: A mediating factor affecting alcohol use practices and problems among lesbian social drinkers. *Journal of Drug Use Issues, 29(1)*, 135-154.

Robinson, P. (Ed.). (1996). *Social groups & identities*. Great Britian: Butterworth-Heinemann.

Rosser, S. (1994). *Women's health–Missing from U.S. medicine*. Bloomimgton, IN: Indiana University Press.

Schroeder, D. S., & Laflin, M. T. (1993). Is there a relationship between self-esteem and drug use? Methodological and statistical limitations of the research. *Journal of Drug Issues, 23(4)*, 645-666.

Sorensen, L. & Roberts, S. (1997). Lesbian uses of and satisfaction with mental health services: Results from Boston lesbian health project. *Journal of Homosexuality, 33*, 35-49.

Stern, P. (1993). *Lesbian health*. Indianapolis, IN: Taylor & Francis.

Sullum, J. (1998). The truth about youth. *Reason, 29*, 21-22.

Tajfel, H. (Ed.). (1978). *Differentiation between social groups: studies in the social psychology of intergroup relations*. New York: Published in cooperation with European Association of Experimental Social Psychology by Academic Press.

United States Department of Health and Human Services. (1996). *National Household Survey on Drug Abuse: Population Estimates 1996*.

Toward a Grounded Theory of Lesbians' Recovery from Addiction

Connie R. Matthews
Peggy Lorah
Jaime Fenton

SUMMARY. This article presents the results of a qualitative study on lesbians' recovery from addiction. The study involved semi-structured interviews with 20 lesbians in recovery from addiction and was analyzed using grounded theory method. The central theme that emerged was self-acceptance, both as a lesbian and as a recovering alcoholic/addict, with considerable interaction between the two. Categories that contributed to this theme were learning to recover, relationships with other people, and relationship with something bigger than self. The discussion addresses how this information can be used to assist lesbians trying to recover from addiction. *[Article copies available for a fee from The Haworth Document Delivery Service: 1-800-HAWORTH. E-mail address: <docdelivery@haworthpress.com> Website: <http://www.HaworthPress.com> © 2005 by The Haworth Press, Inc. All rights reserved.]*

Connie R. Matthews teaches counselor education and coordinates a graduate program in addiction studies at Pennsylvania State University. Peggy Lorah is a student affairs director at Pennsylvania State University. Jaime Fenton is a doctoral student in counseling psychology at Pennsylvania State University.

Address correspondence to: Connie R. Matthews, Department of Counselor Education, Counseling Psychology, and Rehabilitation Services, Pennsylvania State University, University Park, PA 16802 (E-mail: cxm206@psu.edu).

[Haworth co-indexing entry note]: "Toward a Grounded Theory of Lesbians' Recovery from Addiction." Matthews, Connie R., Peggy Lorah, and Jaime Fenton. Co-published simultaneously in *Journal of Lesbian Studies* (Harrington Park Press, an imprint of The Haworth Press, Inc.) Vol. 9, No. 3, 2005, pp. 57-68; and: *Making Lesbians Visible in the Substance Use Field* (ed: Elizabeth Ettorre) Harrington Park Press, an imprint of The Haworth Press, Inc., 2005, pp. 57-68. Single or multiple copies of this article are available for a fee from The Haworth Document Delivery Service [1-800-HAWORTH, 9:00 a.m. - 5:00 p.m. (EST). E-mail address: docdelivery@haworthpress.com].

Available online at http://www.haworthpress.com/web/JLS
© 2005 by The Haworth Press, Inc. All rights reserved.
doi:10.1300/J155v09n03_06

KEYWORDS. Lesbians, addiction, recovery, chemical dependency, substance abuse

Although it is difficult to get an accurate estimate of the rate of alcohol abuse and alcoholism in the lesbian population, the existing literature does suggest that the rate of alcoholism among lesbians is greater than the rate among heterosexual women, that use does not decline with age as it does among heterosexual women, and that lesbians experience more problems associated with drinking than do heterosexual women (Abbott, 1998; Bux, 1996; Cabaj, 1996; McKirnan & Peterson, 1989). Fourteen percent of the lesbians in Bradford, Ryan, and Rothblum's (1994) national lesbian health care study reported being worried about their drinking. In a review of three large studies of lesbian health concerns, Cochran, Bybee, Gage, and Mays (1996) reported rates of alcohol problems among lesbians ranging from 13.7% to 18.7%.

Despite evidence that lesbians experience rates of addiction and associated problems that are higher than among heterosexual women, there is very little research on how they recover from addiction. The small amount of information that is available tends to address barriers to recovery for lesbians (e.g., Bushway, 1991; Hall, 1994; Nicoloff & Stiglitz, 1987). Although this is important as it speaks to unique concerns that should be addressed in addiction treatment, it is equally important to explore the factors that are facilitative of recovery for lesbians. The purpose of this qualitative study is to examine, in an in-depth and narrative fashion, the factors that women who self-identify as lesbian and in recovery from addiction have found helpful in their recovery from addiction. The ultimate goal is to be able to provide better, more informed addiction treatment for this population.

METHOD

Procedures

Because there is so little existing empirical research on how lesbians recover from addiction, we chose a qualitative approach. Qualitative research is especially appropriate for exploratory work that is inductive, aimed at gathering rich, descriptive information for theory building (Merriam, 2002). Participants were recruited through purposeful sampling, which is characteristic of qualitative research (Patton, 1990). The criteria for participation were that individuals be at least 18 years of age, self-identify as lesbian, and be in recovery from alcohol and/or other drugs for at least a year. The one-year minimum time in recovery was established to allow enough time for participants to be able to reflect on the process and to insure that recovery was well enough established that participation in the study would not disrupt it.

Recruitment notices were posted on listservs likely to be read by lesbians and sent to lesbian, gay, and bisexual community or health centers, including some gay Alcoholics Anonymous groups. Women who responded to the announcement were sent a Letter of Informed Consent, which described the study in more detail and allowed participants to formally indicate their consent. Along with the letter was a Background Questionnaire for participants to complete, which asked basic demographic information and length of time in recovery. Once the signed consent form was returned, one of the researchers contacted the participant to schedule a telephone interview, which was audiotaped with the participant's permission. Although telephone interviews can sometimes be limited due to less natural conversational context than face-to-face interviews, lower response rates, and greater participant caution with respect to sensitive material, they are also more resource-efficient and allow for greater uniformity in delivery (Shuy, 2002). The material in this study was sensitive; however, all participants volunteered to be involved, so response rates and sensitivity of material were less pressing concerns and conversational rapport can be improved with adequate preparation (Rubin & Rubin, 1995). Thus, the ability to substantially increase the number and geographic diversity of the sample made telephone interviews the preferred approach for this study.

A series of open-ended questions was used to prompt discussion; however, participants were encouraged to add to or expand upon any topic. Prompt questions encouraged participants to talk about the experiences, people, or situations they believed were helpful to them in their recovery efforts. We asked about such things as formal treatment, involvement in twelve-step programs, role of family and friends, and advice for counselors, as well as other lesbians trying to recover. The interviewers also pursued areas that seemed meaningful as they arose. Interviews began and ended with very broad questions that gave participants an opportunity to address whatever they thought was important. A question about spirituality was added to the protocol after several initial participants spoke of its importance to them in response to the opening question. One of the strengths of qualitative inquiry is that it is an emergent process (Armino & Hultgren, 2002).

The audiotapes of the interviews were transcribed by a professional transcriptionist. To verify the accuracy of the transcription, an individual not otherwise connected to the project reconciled each of the written transcriptions with the audiotape. In addition, the written transcription was sent to the participant for review to be sure that her comments were accurately recorded.

Participants

Thirty women responded to the recruitment announcement and were sent a letter of informed consent and a background questionnaire. Nine women did not return the completed forms and one failed to respond to attempts to schedule an interview, leaving a final sample of twenty participants. Ages ranged from 25 to 55. In response to a question about ethnicity, the majority (16) self-identified as Caucasian, White, or European American; two identified as African American; and two identified as Jewish. Eleven participants reported being in recovery from both alcohol and other drugs; eight reported being in recovery from alcohol alone; one reported being in recovery from other drugs but not alcohol. Participants lived in seven different states, representing the west coast, midwest, mid-Atlantic, and northeast regions of the United States.

Researchers

The research team consisted of three White women, two of whom identify as lesbian and one of whom identifies as heterosexual. All three identify as feminist. None of the researchers is in recovery from addiction; however, the first two authors worked in the addictions field for a combined 27 years prior to moving into academia.

RESULTS

Data Analysis

A grounded theory approach was used to analyze the written transcripts. The goal of grounded theory is to build theory inductively from data that is anchored in people's experiences (Merriam, 2002). The focus is discovery. We began with open coding (Strauss & Corbin, 1998). All three researchers independently read through the transcripts to determine what themes would emerge from the data. We met to compare themes and to generate tentative categories. Then, using constant comparison, we went back to the transcripts to determine the degree to which the categories continued to hold together and to begin defining the properties of the categories. As we did that we began the process of axial coding (Strauss & Corbin, 1998), or finding sub-themes within the categories and the interrelationship between sub-categories and categories. Again, we continued with constant comparison, moving between the data in the transcripts and discussions with each other. We continued this process until we reached consensus on the categories and theory that were emerging. We generally agreed on the concepts that emerged; however, in our independent work we sometimes used different language to explain what we found. We would discuss this until we all three could agree on the labels and definitions that we used to describe the data. This brought us to selective coding (Strauss & Corbin, 1998), or pulling together the categories into meaningful relationships with each other.

Categories That Emerged

Central Phenomenon. The overarching category, or central phenomenon (Strauss & Corbin, 1998), to emerge from the data was the importance of self-acceptance, both as a lesbian and as a recovering alcoholic and/or addict. This was a theme that ran throughout the transcripts, even though there were no prompt questions that addressed it. The women repeatedly indicated that learning to accept themselves was fundamental to their ongoing recovery. At the same time, recovery was necessary in order for them to develop this self-acceptance. The progression appears to be that recovery must come first, that this is a prerequisite for the openness and self-reflection necessary to explore issues related to sexual orientation and one's history as an addict. Without recovery, such exploration tends to lead to increased use of chemicals as a coping mechanism. ". . . No matter what you face by way of homophobia the recovery has to come first. We [other lesbians and gay men in recovery] can give you the strength to face and deal with that stuff. . . ." Thus, the journey begins with recovery. At the same time, self-acceptance is fundamental to maintaining recovery over time. One participant described it this way: "But since I have been in recovery I have gotten a lot more comfortable with who I am. . . . My coming out and my sobriety are so directly linked . . . intertwined and they feed off of each other . . . and that is a big part of who I am today." Another participant advised lesbians working toward recovery to do "everything that one can do to help you feel good about yourself and who you are ... and keep trying to build your toolbox of available tools to help you feel good about yourself." Self-acceptance was clearly the most critical factor in long term recovery, cutting across all of the themes.

Contributing Categories. Three broad categories contribute to the development and maintenance of self-acceptance. These are *learning to recover, relationships with other people,* and *relationship with something bigger than self. Learning to recover* refers to those situations, people and things that helped the participant learn what she needed to develop a healthy recovery. Several concepts emerged. The most prominent was the role of Alcoholics Anonymous (A.A.), with a few also mentioning Narcotics Anonymous (N.A.). Learning the program and working the twelve steps offered a new way of living one's life without chemicals. "... People that aren't alcoholics or not addicts think A.A. is all about drinking but it is really not.... It is about how you live your life." This also provided an avenue for making connections with people who were sober, people they could learn from. "I think the identification is helpful to be around people who have more clean time than me and they are an example and a sort of source of wonderment...." "What was probably most helpful to me was I was actually twelve-stepped by another lesbian." Participants mentioned limitations of A.A., but overall they found it crucial to getting sober. Most of the participants had some involvement with women's and/or gay meetings. Values they saw in these specialized meetings primarily centered on being with people who were like themselves. "... Being with other women, we all seem to understand each other and it is a different kind of fellowship, like sisterhood...." They also provided a means for connecting with the lesbian or women's community in ways that did not involve alcohol or other drugs. In some instances, gender had more salience and in some instances sexual orientation was more important. Sometimes it was a matter of availability of meetings. There was a range of personal preferences with respect to whether an individual woman preferred women's, gay, or mixed meetings. They seemed to get something different from each and seemed drawn to what they needed most. Several women also mentioned the importance of sponsors providing one-on-one connection. "... The biggest help to me has been at many meetings working with my sponsor and ... the twelve steps. It has really helped me get to know myself." There were also a few comments about the inherent heterosexism of A.A. in requiring same sex sponsors to alleviate sexual attraction. However, this was something participants seemed able to work with.

Two other concepts that were important in *learning recovery* were working with therapists and engaging in self-care. Although many of the participants had worked with a therapist, the focus on therapy was clearly secondary to the focus on A.A. When the women did work with a therapist it was important that the therapist both understand and accept their sexual orientation. "I think it is important that you don't have a counselor who still thinks about being homosexual as some kind of deviant DSM classification." It was likewise important that the therapist both understand and accept her addiction. "When you are first starting out in recovery . . . you want a therapist or a counselor that knows the deal because it is such a bizarre disease." Because the interaction of sexual orientation and addiction was such a fundamental part of self-acceptance, if a therapist was to be helpful she or he had to be able to effectively address both issues. Some, although not all, participants found it helpful if the therapist was either a lesbian, in recovery, or both. ". . . The counselor I am seeing now is a lesbian and she is in the program, so I think that helps me feel like she can understand." Another important concept of *learning recovery* that was directly linked to self-acceptance was engaging in self-care. This concept took on different meanings. Sometimes it involved finding other activities to fill one's time; sometimes it involved re-channeling survival skills learned in addiction to promote recovery; often it involved addressing a co-occurring mental illness, frequently with medication. Learning to value appropriate medication, as opposed to self-medicating with alcohol or other drugs, seemed to be an important piece of this. This also meant finding A.A. meetings that would respect this.

A second major category related to self-acceptance involved *relationships with other people*. The need to renegotiate the relationship with the family of origin was addressed frequently. This pertained as much or more to the addiction as to sexual orientation. Although we made a point when asking about family to address family broadly as "however you define that," participants went immediately to family of origin in responding. Some spoke of their family's support, especially in remembering or celebrating sobriety milestones or attending meetings; however, others spoke of ongoing addiction in their family that had to be negotiated. Sexual orientation was also something that had to be negotiated with families. Some participants reported that their families were more accepting than not of both their recovery status and their sexual orientation, but that this acceptance seemed based on not talking about either. "My mom and dad are really good about watching my daughter while I attend meetings . . . although they don't particularly care to hear the details about the A.A. program." The same participant later commented about her sexual orientation, "They would prefer to hear nothing about that, but . . . they are not . . . completely unaccepting. . . . They are just so Donna Reed [1950s U.S. television star who portrayed the perfect wife and mother]. . . . They would just prefer not to deal with it." Some participants included their partners when addressing family. When this occurred they made a point of indicating whether or not the partner was also in recovery. Most partners were supportive of them in their recovery, although in some instances this was something that had to be worked out as a couple. A few participants mentioned leaving relationships that seemed detrimental to their recovery.

Another important concept in this category was the importance of making connections with friendship networks. Creating support networks was an important part of recovery. Some specifically mentioned the importance of having a social network of people who did not use chemicals. Some addressed the centrality of the gay bar to that community and the need to find other avenues for connection. "I mean unfortunately even today the bar culture is still alive and well . . . where a lot of people still think they have to go to meet somebody. . . ." These social networks had a family-like quality to them. Participants often referred to them as family, even though they did not address them when asked about family. ". . . We develop our own families . . . support networks. If you ask people questions about their family you have to be able to understand that that may not mean families of origin, that it is probably a network that is there that has to be recognized." The women spoke of building relationships of trust and ways in which people in these networks helped each other. A.A. was often a mechanism for creating these networks and this was an area where gay meetings or women's meetings sometimes played a role. ". . . The lesbian meeting was more intimate. We developed a lot more informal supports, too, because I think we were minorities and we had . . . a lot of friendships and stuff, not just around A.A."

Another concept associated with *relationships with other people* had to do with managing multiple identities. These women were not simply lesbians or recovering addicts; they were both. Each identity influenced how they experienced the other. Furthermore, they were women. Thus, gender was salient. Some also spoke of racial or ethnic influences. To a large extent, this concept referred to participants being both lesbian and in recovery. Participants spoke from two different perspectives. Some were comfortable with the A.A. teachings that stress focusing on the similarities (as alcoholics) rather than on the differences. ". . . It doesn't really matter if you are gay, straight, Black, White, you still have the same disease, so try not to think of yourself as so unique." Others needed to be able to address sexual orientation and/or gender along with the addiction. "I really don't know what I would have done without the gay meeting. . . . I have met other gay people and I can bring my gay issues to this meeting where I can't bring my gay issues to any other meeting." At the same time, the concept of managing multiple identities seemed to be most salient to those individuals who also had yet another aspect to their identity that they wanted or needed to address. Specifically, the Jewish women spoke about the emphasis on Christianity that is present in many A.A. meetings and the African American women spoke of the racism that they experience. "I don't know why that [The Lord's Prayer] was there because they always said it was not a religious program, but yet this prayer–that was clearly something that wasn't . . . part of the Jewish or even Muslim people or anybody that didn't go to church." It is important to stress that in finding self-acceptance and maintaining sobriety, these were things the women were able to overcome; however, they are issues that they did need to address.

A final concept related to *relationships with other people* addressed geographic issues. This did not seem to be a major concept but was one addressed by a number of women. Some of the participants spoke of the advantages of living in a place where they had access to a lesbian community and/or where being lesbian was more accepted by the general population. ". . . Where I live there is a fairly large lesbian community, so that is a great resource." Others spoke of the lack of such access or the greater stigma attached to being lesbian because of where they lived.

The third major category interacting with self-acceptance was finding a *relationship with something bigger than self*. There were two concepts related to this, a struggle with traditional religion and redefining spirituality. The former was generally discussed in conjunction with the latter. "I pray differently. I look at God differently. I have more of a relationship with God rather than fearing God like I did growing up." This was a very important concept to the women in this study. "You can't stay sober without it [spirituality]. You can't do the tough stuff without it." It was an area that was added to the interview questions after the early respondents repeatedly and poignantly addressed it without us asking. The women were clear in separating spirituality from religion. Indeed, it was this distinction that was important. Some participants referred to God; others did not. Many spoke of a period of separation from any sense of spirituality due to the homophobia and sexism present in the religions in which they were raised. ". . . It is kind of a surprise. I guess I never really thought I would be like this. I never thought I would be spiritual.... It has been a great thing and it has been a huge gift." Being able to redefine spirituality and draw strength from accepting something outside of themselves helped their journeys to self-acceptance, which in turn helped them on their spiritual journeys. The A.A. concept of higher power helped some women with this process, although some also struggled with what they perceived as an emphasis on Christianity in some A.A. groups. One woman defined her spirituality as more of an "inner power" than a higher power. "... Not necessarily a higher power but an inner power is what I should be calling it . . . more of an inner voice or inner spirit that if I listen to things usually turn out okay."

DISCUSSION

Although we did not address the issue directly in our interview questions, the theme to emerge as the central phenomenon in this study clearly was self-acceptance. Closely linked to this was the interrelationship between sexual orientation and addiction. The women in this study reported an ongoing and somewhat complex relationship between their addiction and their sexual orientation. Struggles with accepting their sexual orientation fed their addiction, as they used chemicals as a means of coping with something they could not face. At the same time, the consistent message was that sobriety was necessary to face and accept their sexual orientation. Equally consistent was the realization that self-acceptance was crucial for ongoing sobriety.

This relationship makes sense when one considers the role of shame in both processes. Shame has long been associated with addiction (Potter-Efron, 2002). Working toward overcoming shame is an important aspect of addiction treatment and involvement in twelve-step programs (Brown, 1991). This may at least partially explain why A.A. played such a large role in early recovery for these women. Likewise, shame has also been linked to the internalized homophobia that is a product of heterosexism in society (Neisen, 1993). Addiction treatment programs typically cover the shame associated with addiction, yet for lesbian women this addresses only part of the problem. It is equally important that programs address the shame associated with internalized homophobia if they are to be effective in helping lesbian addicts become fully self-accepting.

Closely linked to both the development and maintenance of self-acceptance for the women in this study was redefining spirituality. It was important to them to be able to draw strength from something beyond themselves, which they may or may not refer to as God. At the same time, religion that felt punishing exacerbated shame rather than supporting recovery. A.A. and many treatment programs incorporate spirituality into the process of recovery. When this was truly an open and flexible concept of "higher power" it facilitated the process of rediscovering and redefining spirituality. When "higher power" was interpreted as a/the Christian God, the participants were more apt to struggle. This is something that addiction counselors must address if they are to help lesbians to acquire self-acceptance and recovery.

Likewise, it is vital to help lesbians make connections with support systems that will respect and honor both their sexual orientation and addiction. This is particularly critical given the role of the gay bar and other alcohol and drug related functions in the lesbian/gay/bisexual community. Because lesbians in recovery often have multiple personal identities, it is important to pay attention to which identities seem most salient at any given time. For the women in this study, that sometimes was gender, sexual orientation, ethnicity, and addiction. Rather than make assumptions as to which this might be, it is important to assess this individually. There are multiple levels on which lesbians in recovery must overcome stigma and discrimination. It is vital that the complexity of these interactions be incorporated into treatment.

REFERENCES

Abbott, L. J. (1998). The use of alcohol by lesbians: A review and research agenda. *Substance Use and Misuse, 33*, 2647-2663.

Armino, J. L., & Hultgren, F. H. (2002). Breaking out from the shadow: The question of criteria in qualitative research. *Journal of College Student Development, 43*, 446-460.

Bradford, J., Ryan, C., & Rothblum, E. D. (1994). National lesbian health care survey: Implications for mental health care. *Journal of Consulting and Clinical Psychology, 62*, 228-242.

Brown, H. M. (1991). Shame and relapse issues with the chemically dependent client. *Alcoholism Treatment Quarterly, 8*(3), 77-82.

Bushway, D. J. (1991). Chemical dependency treatment for lesbians and their families: The feminist challenge. In C. Bepko (Ed.), *Feminism and addiction* (pp. 161-172). New York: Haworth.

Bux, D. A., Jr. (1996). The epidemiology of problem drinking in gay men and lesbians: A critical review. *Clinical Psychology Review, 16*, 277-298.

Cabaj, R. P. (1996). Substance abuse in gay men, lesbians, and bisexuals. In R. P. Cabaj & T. S. Stein (Eds.), *Textbook of homosexuality and mental health* (pp. 783-799). Washington, D.C.: American Psychiatric Press, Inc.

Cochran, S. D., Bybee, D., Gage, S., & Mays, V. (1996). Prevalence of HIV-Related self-reported sexual behaviors, sexually transmitted diseases, and problems with drugs and alcohol in three large surveys of lesbian and bisexual women: A look into a segment of the community. *Women's health: Research on gender, behavior, and policy, 2,* 11-33.

Hall, J. M. (1994). Lesbians recovering from alcohol problems: An ethnographic study of Health care experiences. *Nursing research, 43,* 238-244.

McKirnan, D. J., & Peterson, P. L. (1989). Alcohol and drug use among homosexual men and women: Epidemiology and population characteristics. *Addictive Behaviors, 14,* 545-553.

Neisen, J. H. (1993). Healing from cultural victimization: Recovery from shame due to heterosexism. *Journal of Gay & Lesbian Psychotherapy, 2* (1), 49-63.

Merriam, S. B. (2002). Introduction to qualitative research. In S. B. Merriam and Associates (Eds.), *Qualitative research in practice: Examples for discussion and analysis.* San Francisco, CA: Jossey-Bass.

Nicoloff, L. K., & Stiglitz, E. A. (1987). Lesbian alcoholism: Etiology, treatment, and recovery. In Boston Lesbian Psychologies Collective (Eds.), *Lesbian psychologies Explorations and challenges* (pp. 283-293). Urbana, IL: University of Illinois Press.

Patton, M. Q. (1990). *Qualitative evaluation and research methods* (2nd Ed.). Newbury Park, CA: Sage.

Potter-Efron, R. (2002). *Shame, guilt, and alcoholism: Treatment issues in clinical practice* (2nd Ed.). New York: Haworth Press.

Rubin, H. J., & Rubin, I. S. (1995). *Qualitative interviewing: The art of hearing data.* Thousand Oaks, CA: Sage.

Strauss, A., & Corbin, J. (1998). *Basics of qualitative research: Techniques and procedures for developing grounded theory.* Thousand Oaks, CA: Sage.

Shuy, R. W. (2002). In-person versus telephone interviewing. In J. F. Gubrium & J. A. Holstein (Eds.), *Handbook of interview research: Context and method* (pp. 537-555). Thousand Oaks, CA: Sage.

Labelling Out:
The Personal Account of an Ex-Alcoholic Lesbian Feminist

Patsy Staddon

SUMMARY. In this paper, I look at my past alcohol dependency from a political as well as personal perspective. I consider the problems caused in my life and that of other lesbians by alcohol abuse, outdated treatment methods and self-help organizations such as AA, which misrepresent social factors leading to alcohol abuse. I focus on a series of themes: the personal and political; lesbian bar styles; alternative realities; lesbian problem drinking; problems facing lesbians in treatment and engaging with Alcoholics Anonymous; treatment as it often is and treatment as it should be. *[Article copies available for a fee from The Haworth Document Delivery Service: 1-800-HAWORTH. E-mail address: <docdelivery@haworthpress.com> Website: <http://www.HaworthPress.com> © 2005 by The Haworth Press, Inc. All rights reserved.]*

Patsy Staddon, BA(Hons.), MSc, is a feminist and a lesbian. She is currently a PhD student in sociology at the University of Plymouth where she is researching issues of women's alcohol use, misuse, and treatment in the U.K., from the perspective of an ex-alcoholic.

Address correspondence to: Patsy Staddon, Postgraduate Student, University of Plymouth, Faculty of Social Science and Business, School of Sociology, Politics and Law, Drake Circus, Devon, UK (E-mail: patsy.staddon@blueyonder.co.uk).

[Haworth co-indexing entry note]: "Labelling Out: The Personal Account of an Ex-Alcoholic Lesbian Feminist." Staddon, Patsy. Co-published simultaneously in *Journal of Lesbian Studies* (Harrington Park Press, an imprint of The Haworth Press, Inc.) Vol. 9, No. 3, 2005, pp. 69-78; and: *Making Lesbians Visible in the Substance Use Field* (ed: Elizabeth Ettorre) Harrington Park Press, an imprint of The Haworth Press, Inc., 2005, pp. 69-78. Single or multiple copies of this article are available for a fee from The Haworth Document Delivery Service [1-800-HAWORTH, 9:00 a.m. - 5:00 p.m. (EST). E-mail address: docdelivery@haworthpress.com].

Available online at http://www.haworthpress.com/web/JLS
© 2005 by The Haworth Press, Inc. All rights reserved.
doi:10.1300/J155v09n03_07

KEYWORDS. Alcohol abuse, 'feminist' treatment, lesbian survival

Being drunk . . . it's a brazen refusal to be quiet, well-behaved and ladylike . . . femininity . . . relies on, is defined by, inhibition. (Lawson, 2000)

THE PERSONAL AND THE POLITICAL

I left alcohol abuse behind when I saw my individual distress in the light of wider cultural phenomena. My personal history is also a political one. I am a 60-year-old British lesbian and ex-alcoholic. Without the feminist movement and lesbian and gay civil rights in the 1970s, I would not be alive today. Being out as a lesbian and recovered alcoholic is my declaration of independence as a living human being. Wearing these labels has given me courage, but these labels also limit the ways in which other people perceive me.

When I first discovered alcohol, I found it liberating. There was a new person inside myself–witty, confident and capable. Without alcohol, I felt a nonentity. Before alcohol, I wanted to fly airplanes, explore jungles, express new ideas and change the world. But, those possibilities were closed for a girl in 1950s Britain. During my twenty-eight years of drinking, I could only get glimpses of my real self. I came to believe what I was told: that my drinking problem was a personal, moral weakness. No one, not even myself, thought it could be related to being a woman. When I was admitted to a Twelve Step specialist day treatment center 16 years ago, patients and staff told me I had a disease for which I was not at fault, but that I was responsible for its consequences. By that time, I had been drinking chaotically for many years. My life was out of control. The one simple explanation was that I was an alcoholic. Grateful for the new label, I would have liked to have believed everything they told me.

At the time, I didn't know many people who had given up destructive drinking on their own, although I knew they existed (Hall, Bolsted & Hamblett, 2001; Ragge, 1998; Prochaska et al., 1983). I too had managed to stop drinking on my own. This was during the six weeks before I entered the Twelve Step day center. This was a result of my finding lesbian friends who were neither drinkers nor judgmental about my drinking. They introduced me to women who were interested in feminist issues, and made me feel welcome. For the first time in twenty-eight years, I could manage without alcohol. I chose to go into treatment because I thought it would help me to stay sober. It was not totally negative, given that I learned some useful techniques for relating to others and understanding myself. The personal space gained by attending such a treatment center was valuable for me. But, the Twelve Step philosophy embedded in the treatment program was difficult for me to accept because I was beginning to question the values of a patriarchal, heterosexist society. In my view, this philosophy upheld such a society and although I was frightened, I was determined to reject it. How could I accept a philosophy which in my view devalued what I loved most in myself, for example, my independence of thought and openness to new ideas?

Gradually, I was able to build a new life without alcohol and wear a different label besides alcoholic. I was a lesbian feminist–a label I embraced. Still, I was desperate to make sense of my life. Why had I become an alcoholic? Could my experiences be explained sociologically through a perspective that focuses on the group as the basic unit of analysis and asks the observer to take a concentrated look at social phenomena (Gusfield, 1996)? Perhaps, I thought. Through a sociological lens and as a lesbian feminist, I saw that I was damaged by growing up with heterosexist expectations about how I should look, act and feel. But, I still found it hard to connect my earlier need to drink to oblivion with my having felt a social misfit for most of my life. Drinking had been a coping mechanism when I felt that I didn't fit in the heterosexist world. Coming out gave me the opportunity to fit into my newly discovered lesbian world.

LESBIAN BARS: LOOKING HEALTHY "BEING COOL"

As lesbians, we have had to build our own environments in a world that is structured by and for heterosexuals, and the gay bar is "where you can meet your friends . . . be who you really are" (Jo, aged 34).[1] In a heterosexist world, with its talk of husbands and families, we may never feel that we fit in. We need places where we can grumble to friends, show off a bit and relax. In lesbian bars, we are not outsiders and can take pleasure in our differences. Style is an expression of this pleasure, as we create new lesbian attire and ways of behaving with fascinating results. Lesbian style is being at home in your body, your clothes and knowing who you are. "It's about being at ease, in your element, knowing what's expected. The ultimate cool is when everyone knows you. If it's a new place, it's important to know the etiquette . . . how things are done" (Caro, aged 46).

I've noticed that drinking a lot of alcohol in lesbian bars is less common than earlier when I had drinking problems. It's the idea that nowadays we can look good with a soft drink–"It's not so much of a sex symbol thing. It's looking healthy that looks cool" (Caro, aged 46). Where I come from lesbians have to travel a bit to find a lesbian bar–probably further than heterosexuals do to find a straight one. So the car and driving license are precious. "It's the het (sic) girls who go out in gangs getting plastered now. It's sort of respectable for them. But not many of us would have more than a pint . . . during a night out" (Jen, aged 29). Once you know the crowd and local etiquette, you fit in whatever you drink. In a new setting, you may feel a stranger, but less so than you would in a straight bar.

ALTERNATIVE REALITIES (OR, WHOSE BODY IS IT ANYWAY?)

Heavy consumption of alcohol may have a particular relevance for some lesbians, although they may not drink in bars. Drunkenness may be a gateway to sexual and spiritual freedom rather than an unhealthy and deplorable activity. Women, encouraged to be sedate, at least in public, often lack a suitable physical and psychic arena for expressing difference and sheer pleasure (Ettorre, 1992). Other cultures, in particular agrarian ones, often have a different attitude to drunkenness in women (Harvey, 1994). Additionally, a substantial number of women perceive alcohol as an aphrodisiac (Wilsnack, 1984) in a patriarchal society that fears women's power over their own pleasure, and this can also apply to lesbians (Sjoo and Mor, 1987). Western societies lack rituals of spiritual expression which remain a normal part of life in the developing societies (Harvey, 1994). It could be said that exploring the self is a common need, whether this is achieved by prayer, meditation, shooting up, or drumming in the moonlight. Perhaps, we're wrong to assume that drunkenness in women always requires medical attention and control through deviant labels such as "slut" or "whore." It may be an appropriate expression of one's current spiritual and emotional needs (Ettorre, 1997).

LESBIAN PROBLEM DRINKING

Being a member of a minority is stressful and lesbians more than heterosexual women tend to feel the ill effects of a value system based on heteronormativity. This is especially true for those who have felt unable to live open lives. Homophobia creates depression, a major factor among women who misuse alcohol (Kendler et al., 1993). Lesbians can become unhappy and depressed because of their families' incomprehension of their lesbianism, their inability to share in the lives of heterosexual workmates and their being ignored by health providers and educators. If the lesbian scene is not for them, they may experience loneliness. For them, alcohol can be exciting and pleasurable: "You get what you need from drugs" (respondent quoted in Raine, 2001 p. 23). It would not be surprising if some lesbians abuse alcohol and feel unable to control their alcohol intake. Some research indicates that stigma, alienation, discrimination, and the cultural importance of bars place lesbians more at risk of developing problems with alcohol than heterosexual women (Rule, 2003). Other research supports the idea that lesbian drinking is more problematic than that of heterosexual women. (Jaffe, Clance, Nichols, & Ernshoff, 2000)

PROBLEMS FACING LESBIANS IN ALCOHOL TREATMENT

Chaotic drinking occurs for all women, lesbian or straight, but being a lesbian and drunk may be a less shameful experience. Some lesbians may be scornful of traditionally feminine behaviour such as looking smart and tidy, not being noisy in public and not being seen to be affected by alcohol. This attitude is likely to make it easier to admit to yourself and your friends that you have a problem with alcohol, since you are not perceived as being socially disgraced in the same way. Unfortunately, this advantage is soon cancelled out when you go for treatment. As lesbians, we may be suspicious about the motivation behind what current mental health treatments offer. Where women are concerned, "the clinician . . . will find little in the way of sound empirical guidance" (Braiker, 1984, p. 349). Yet lack of "sound empirical guidance" has not prevented the medical profession from putting its ideas about lesbians into practice. It is less than fifty years since it was considered appropriate in the U.K. to administer electric shock treatment to homosexual patients to "cure" them. The *BMJ* recently, and belatedly, published an apology for this on behalf of the medical profession (MacDonald, 2004).

Lesbians are right to still be concerned about a mental health service that does not make adequate provision for women patients, let alone those of sexual, racial or ethnic minorities. When lesbians seek help for alcohol issues and are open about their sexuality, the labels "lesbian" and "alcoholic" indicate to clinical staff that they are socially dysfunctional: "Conformity rather than being viewed as a social accomplishment is elevated to the status of 'health'" (Pearson, 1975, quoted by Kitzinger 1987, p. 33). Perceived as doubly deviant in their substance use and their sexuality (Roberts, 1985; Bridget, 2001), lesbians "are much less likely to present to these services for a variety of reasons . . . [including] . . . fear of their sexuality being pathologized if they do present" (Malley, 2001).

AA: YET ANOTHER ALTERNATIVE REALITY

In my view, these difficulties explain why some lesbians make use of the Alcoholics Anonymous (AA) network. The sense of being in your own secure environment, experienced in lesbian bars, may be felt when mingling in AA "Rooms," where people with similar life experiences drop their guard. In lesbian bars, lesbians do not need to apologize for who they are. In the same way, people in AA meetings do not need to explain who they are. However, frequently they apologize for their behaviour. In my experience, there is an uneasy relationship between being lesbian, celebrating difference from heteronormativity, and being alcoholic, which sees alcoholism as a "disease." Possibly, this is easier for lesbians who see themselves as "alcoholics" first and lesbians second. The AA world of acceptance and perpetual dependence may feel strange to lesbians who have already had to fight society in order to accept their sexuality. AA newcomers are termed "babies": one never grows up and recovers. Instead, one is forever "in recovery." Members are warned: you will drink if you leave AA. Frequent suicides are often passed off with explanations like "the alcohol got 'em," and these serve as warnings to others to be humble, obedient, selfless (Ragge 1998, p. 138). Aware of it or not, AA members buy into a limited respectability and acceptance for themselves by being tagged "alcoholic." If they embrace AA membership they are able to avoid a sizeable proportion of blame for drinking. Going to AA meetings implies that they are following the AA Twelve Step program. They accept that they have an incurable, lifelong disease, and are doing their best to deal with it by admitting they are powerless over alcohol. They give up their power to "God as we understand him" (Alcoholics Anonymous, 2002) and follow the Steps while remaining abstinent. If they drink, and confess this in AA, this lapse is described as a "slip." Members are encouraged to "work the Steps" (i.e., to follow the program) rigorously and not to look at specific causes for any slips.

For me, AA is like an open asylum for people who accept that they can't be cured but do their best to behave in ways society requires alcoholics to behave. In one sense this is the opposite of the lesbian and gay world–out and proud. On the other hand, the AA world is similar to our own. Both worlds have obtained a measure of respectability, if not acceptance. Both enrich social diversity and are somewhat visible. But, both are named, owned and controlled by heteronormative society.

TREATMENT AS IT OFTEN IS

In my experience of treatment, I found fear of disapproval to be an important mechanism of social control. Both this fear of disapproval and the additional one of not being understood can affect lesbians in treatment. For example, recently, I interviewed lesbians and bisexual women about their experience of alcohol treatment. With one exception, all reported that because of these fears, they concealed their sexuality throughout treatment. Could this have helped their "recovery"? Are their fears well founded? Perhaps they are, given that staff belittlement of females occurs often in the masculinist environment of alcohol treatment centers (Ettorre, 1997). I found that ridicule, coercion, verbal abuse and contempt were used by psychiatrists, doctors and community psychiatric nurses. In my current research, one lesbian reported that a medical practitioner walked out on a lesbian who admitted her symptoms were linked to heavy alcohol consumption. In another incident, a male psychiatric nurse scorned an important lover relationship for his lesbian patient and reduced her to tears. "I'd never go back there," she said.

The methods employed by AA tend to be used in a number of treatment centers. Overall, the medical model of mental disorder, of which the AA ideology is a part, obscures the social processes that produce and define deviance by locating problems in individual biology (Moncrieff, 1997). A patient's partner may be abusing her or she may have many other problems. However, these problems may be perceived as irrelevant by treatment staff who lack the will to implement change (Bridget, 2001) or consider wider social issues.

TREATMENT AS IT SHOULD BE

In the U.K., some treatment centers have adopted more eclectic and holistic methods, including acupuncture and non-directive counseling, such as the Community Action Against Alcohol and Drugs (CAAAD) project in Bristol and the Gloucestershire Drugs and Alcohol Services (GDAS) project in Cinderford. In a few areas, such as London's Tower Hamlets, substance misuse and domestic abuse agencies work closely with one another. There is provision of specialist services for lesbians with alcohol problems such as the Drug and Alcohol Service for London and the Calderdale service.

Current treatment recommendations for women seeking help with alcohol issues (Staddon, 2003) show that women do best in women-only groups (Raine, 2001; Thom, 1994) with one-to-one counseling and choice of gender of worker (Cameron, 1995); flexible opening hours (Swan, Farber & Campbell, 2004); when their responsibilities as family caretakers are recognized (Raine, 2001; Plant, 1997); and they are allowed to take their children with them into residential treatment (McCaul, 1998). Of course, these issues apply to all women, lesbian, bisexual or heterosexual.

But, in my experience, lesbians have different treatment needs, although the general belief in the treatment world is that lesbians are the same as everyone else and should be treated the same (Bridget, 1994). Bridget (2001) recommends the establishment of a Lesbian/Gay/Bisexual/Transexual Addictions Task Group, which would conduct assessment of needs and then establish services which are friendly to Lesbian/Gay/Bisexual/Transexual people. It would involve a dedicated person to work with members of this group with alcohol/drugs problems. She envisaged "coming off addictions" groups for Lesbian/Gay/Bisexual/Transexual people.

In conclusion, while endorsing the above recommendations, I should like to see a greater awareness of the positive contribution use of alcohol may have in the lives of lesbians. Those who would like to help in the treatment field should free themselves of outdated methods which seek to control rather than empower lesbians. If "getting well" implies adopting a set of prohibitive instructions for day-to-day living then "getting well" may be an unwanted disablement. We must have a wider view on lesbians' alcohol use and abuse if we want to effect changes. Otherwise, for many lesbian alcoholics the bottom of a bottle might still be the safest place to be.

NOTE

1. The quotations used in this section come from a small pilot study that I ran in April 2004, to obtain the views of lesbians in bars in a large city in the southwest of England.

REFERENCES

Alcoholics Anonymous. *Twelve steps and twelve traditions* (Alcoholics Anonymous World Services, Inc., 2002)

Braiker, H.B. (1984). Therapeutic issues in the treatment of alcoholic women in S.C. Wilsnack and L.J. Beckman (Eds.) *Alcohol problems in women* (pp. 349-368) New York, London: Guilford.

Bridget, J. (1994). *Treatment of lesbians with alcohol problems in alcohol services in North West England* Lesbian Information Service.

Bridget, J. (2001). *Lesbians, gay men and alcohol conference report* Alcohol Concern Website.

Cameron, D. (1995). *Liberating solutions.* Jason Aronson Inc.

Ettorre, E. (1997). *Women and alcohol* The Women's Press.

Ettorre, E. (1992). *Women and substance use* New Brunswick, New Jersey: Rutgers University Press.

Gusfield, J.R. (1996). *Contested meanings: The construction of alcohol problems* University of Wisconsin.

Hall, M., Bodenhamer, B.G., Bolsted R., & Hamblett M. (2001). *The structure of personality.* Crown House.

Harvey, P. (1994). Gender, community and confrontation. in M. McDonald (Ed.) *Gender, drink and drugs* pp. 209-233 Oxford, England: Berg Publishers.

Jaffe, C., Clance P.R., Nichols, M.F., Emshoff, J.G. (2000). The prevalence of alcoholism and feelings of alienation in lesbian and heterosexual women *Journal of Gay and Lesbian Psychiatry*, 3, 25-27.

Kendler, K.S., Heath,A.C., Neale, M.C., Kessler, R.C. and Eaves, L.J. (1993). Alcoholism and major depression in women: A twin study of the causes of comorbidity. *Archives of General Psychiatry*, 50, 690-698.

Kitzinger, C. (1987). *The social construction of lesbianism.* Sage Publications.

Lawson, N. (Nov. 12th 2000). "I Drink Therefore I Am." *Observer Newspaper.*

MacDonald, R. (21 February, 2004). *British Medical Journal*, 328, 429.

Malley, M. (2001). *Lesbians, gay men and alcohol conference report* Alcohol Concern Website.

McCaul, M.E. (2004). *Treatment outcomes for women drug abusers for National Institute for Drug Abuse* NIDA Publications on Women's Health and Gender Differences. www.drugabuse.gov/WHGD/WHGDHSR.html April 1998

Moncrieff, J. (Summer, 1997). "The medicalisation of diversity and despondency: An examination of late 20th century psychiatry: psychiatric imperialism: the medicalisation of modern living" *Soundings*, 6 63-72.

Pearson, G. (1975). *The deviant imagination: Psychiatry, social work and social change* London: Macmillan.

Plant, M. (1997). *Women and alcohol.* Free Association Books.

Prochaska J., Di Clemente C. (1983). Stages and processes of self-change in Smoking: Toward an integrative model of change *Journal of Consulting and Clinical Psychology* 5 390-395.

Ragge, K. (1998). *The Real AA* See Sharp Press, Tuscon, AZ.

Raine, P. (2001). *Women's perspectives on drugs and alcohol.* Ashgate Publishing Ltd.

Roberts, H. (1985). *The patient patients: Women and their doctors.* Pandora Press Health Report.
Rule, A. (August 23, 2003). Shocking language, *British Medical Journal* 327, 422.
Sjoo, M. & Mor, B. (1987). *The great cosmic mother* San Francisco: Harper.
Staddon, P. (2003). Women's alcohol dependence: A review of the literature. Report for Avon and Wiltshire (Mental Health) N.H.S. Trust, United Kingdom.
Swan, S., Farber, S. Campbell, D. (September 21, 2004). *Violence in the lives of women in substance abuse treatment: Service and policy implications.* Consortium Publications, *www.womensconsortium.org/pdf/*swan
Thom, B. (1994). Women and alcohol: The emergence of a risk group. In M. McDonald, (Ed.) *Gender, drink and drugs* (pp. 33-54). Oxford: Berg.
Wilsnack, S. (1984). Drinking, sexuality and sexual dysfunction in women. In S.C. Wilsnack & L.J. Beckman, (Eds.) *Alcohol problems in women* (pp. 189-227). NY: Guildford Press.

Lesbian, Gay, and Bisexual Clients' Experiences in Treatment for Addiction

Connie R. Matthews
Mary M. D. Selvidge

SUMMARY. This study examined the extent to which lesbian, gay, and bisexual clients perceived their addiction counselors and treatment programs to be sensitive to issues related to sexual orientation. The experiences they considered most successful were reported as more affirmative than experiences they considered least successful; however, in neither situation were counselors or treatment programs consistently affirmative. *[Article copies available for a fee from The Haworth Document Delivery Service: 1-800-HAWORTH. E-mail address: <docdelivery@haworthpress.com> Website: <http://www.HaworthPress.com> © 2005 by The Haworth Press, Inc. All rights reserved.]*

KEYWORDS. Addiction treatment, substance abuse treatment, chemical dependency treatment, lesbian, gay

---

Connie R. Matthews, PhD, is Assistant Professor of Education and Women's Studies and Coordinator of the Addiction Studies Program at The Pennsylvania State University. Mary M. D. Selvidge, PhD, is a consultant in Birmingham, AL.

Address correspondence to: Connie R. Matthews, Department of Counselor Education, Counseling Psychology, and Rehabilitation Services, 333 CEDAR Building, The Pennsylvania State University, University Park, PA 16802 (E-mail: cxm206@psu.edu).

[Haworth co-indexing entry note]: "Lesbian, Gay, and Bisexual Clients' Experiences in Treatment for Addiction." Matthews, Connie R., and Mary M. D. Selvidge. Co-published simultaneously in *Journal of Lesbian Studies* (Harrington Park Press, an imprint of The Haworth Press, Inc.) Vol. 9, No. 3, 2005, pp. 79-90; and: *Making Lesbians Visible in the Substance Use Field* (ed: Elizabeth Ettorre) Harrington Park Press, an imprint of The Haworth Press, Inc., 2005, pp. 79-90. Single or multiple copies of this article are available for a fee from The Haworth Document Delivery Service [1-800-HAWORTH, 9:00 a.m. - 5:00 p.m. (EST). E-mail address: docdelivery@haworthpress.com].

Available online at http://www.haworthpress.com/web/JLS
© 2005 by The Haworth Press, Inc. All rights reserved.
doi:10.1300/J155v09n03_08

INTRODUCTION

In an extensive review of the literature on the prevalence of problem drinking among lesbians and gay men, Bux (1996) drew four conclusions: He suggested that lesbians and gay men are less likely to abstain from using alcohol than their heterosexual counterparts; that compared to heterosexual men, gay men do not appear to be at greater risk for alcohol related problems; that, conversely, lesbians do appear to be at higher risk for heavy and perhaps abusive drinking than heterosexual women; and that reported recent declines in alcohol use and abuse among gay men may be related to changing community norms in response to the AIDS crisis. He also stressed the importance of chemical dependency treatment programs recognizing and addressing the unique needs of the lesbian, gay, and bisexual (LGB) population.

Lesbians, gay men, and bisexual individuals face concerns related to substance use and abuse that are specific to their situation as sexual minorities. A number of scholars (e.g., Beatty et al., 1999; Israelstam, 1986; Israelstam & Lambert, 1989; Paul, Stall, & Bloomfield, 1991; Ratner, 1993) have discussed some of the issues that are particularly relevant to this population and that impact the way they experience addiction. One important concern is the role of the gay bar in socialization. Although a broader range of activities is available now than in the past, the gay bar still often serves as a gathering place for the community. Other issues can include the process of identity formation and coming out, the stress of being part of a stigmatized minority group, and external homophobia that often leads to internal self-hatred. Estrangement from family and friends, lack of recognition of intimate relationships, social isolation and alienation, spiritual distress, and concerns related to sexual expression are additional factors that are particularly applicable to this population.

A number of researchers (e.g., Beatty et al., 1999; Bux, 1996; Cabaj, 1996; Paul et al., 1991; Schaefer, Evans, & Coleman, 1987; Ubell & Sumberg, 1992) have offered specific recommendations for chemical dependency treatment that is sensitive to the unique concerns of LGB individuals. In addition to the general issues mentioned above, they suggest such things as having staff members who are knowledgeable about the specific issues facing addicted LGB people, assisting clients in striking a healthy balance between the need for caution regarding disclosure of sexual orientation and the openness and honesty that are necessary in a recovery program, and having space where it is safe to be fully open. Likewise, family programs also need to be sensitive to such things as expanded definitions of family and the complexities of relationships with families of origin around issues related to sexual orientation. These authors also stress the necessity of being knowledgeable about referral resources, including familiarity with gay 12-step group meetings, assistance in connecting clients with sponsors who are lesbian, gay, or bisexual and recovering, and screening literature provided by other human service providers to insure that they are affirmative. The presence of openly lesbian, gay, and bisexual staff to serve as role models is also mentioned often. In addition, Bux (1996) stresses that it is vital to recognize that not all of the concerns facing this population are related to sexual orientation. LGB clients experience many of the same issues that all addicted clients experience. It is important to be able to distinguish between those issues that do and those issues that do not pertain to sexual orientation.

Despite this literature that stresses the need for an approach to addiction treatment that is affirmative toward LGB clients, the extent to which addiction counselors and treatment facilities are doing this remains a question. In a study of government-funded treatment facilities in New York City, Hellman, Stanton, Lee, Tytun, and Vachon (1989) found evidence that there was some insensitivity toward this population. Participants in their study reported a lack of information and training in working with LGB clients. They also indicated that counselors frequently failed to address issues related to sexual orientation and were not inclined to refer these clients to other clinicians who might have specialized training. Ratner (1993) reported that 53% of clients entering the Pride Institute, an inpatient treatment facility for lesbian, gay, and bisexual addicts, reported previous inpatient treatment experiences that did not address sexual orientation. Seventy-four percent of the clients in treatment at the Pride Institute for at least five days were abstinent from alcohol and 67% were abstinent from other drugs at 14-month follow-up (Ratner, Kosten, & McLellan, 1991, as cited in Cabaj, 1997).

There is a need to examine further the extent to which substance abuse treatment facilities are being responsive to their lesbian, gay, and bisexual clients and the effect this has on the treatment experience. Matthews, Selvidge, and Fisher (2005) looked at the attitudes and behaviors that all LGB clients will identify as such. They found that gender, years of experience as an addiction counselor, counselor sexual orientation, counselor attitudes toward lesbians and gays, and a non-heterosexist organizational climate predicted the degree to which counselors reported attitudes and behaviors that were affirmative toward clients they knew were lesbian, gay, or bisexual. Although this gives us some information about factors that might influence addiction counselors to practice affirmatively, it nonetheless represents counselors' own self-perceptions.

The present study asks lesbian, gay, and bisexual individuals who had been clients their perceptions of the degree to which addiction counselors and treatment facilities displayed attitudes and behaviors that were affirmative. There were two primary research questions. The first was descriptive–to what extent do former clients report that their addiction counselors and treatment facilities engaged in practices that were affirmative toward them as lesbian, gay, or bisexual clients? The second research question compared the responses participants gave for treatment experiences that they considered most successful with those that they considered least successful (when clients had more than one treatment experience). Were there differences between the experiences considered most successful and those considered least successful in the degree to which the counselors and treatment facilities engaged in practices that were affirmative toward lesbian, gay, and bisexual clients?

METHOD

Participants

Participants were individuals who self-identified as lesbian, gay, or bisexual and in recovery from alcohol and/or drug addiction for at least one year. A total of 71 individuals responded to the online survey; however, 12 failed to complete enough information to be included in analyses and 1 indicated that s/he was not in recovery. This left a sample of 58 participants. Participants represented 22 different states and all geographic regions in the United States; four participants were from outside the United States.

The sample was predominantly White (n = 50; 86.2%), with one or two participants each indicating African American, Asian/Pacific Islander, Hispanic, Indian, or other. Thirty participants were female (51.7%), 26 were male (44.8%), and 2 were male-to-female transgender (3.4%). Ages ranged from 22 to 63, with a mean of 40 (SD = 9.91). Fifty participants indicated that they were in recovery from alcohol abuse, with time in recovery ranging from 1 to 25 years (M = 8.9; SD = 5.3). Forty-four participants reported being in recovery from drug abuse, with time in recovery ranging from 1 to 22 years (M = 8.7; SD = 5.0). Participants were asked to indicate how many treatment experiences they had in inpatient, outpatient, and intensive outpatient/partial hospitalization programs. Thirty-five participants reported a mean of 1.2 inpatient experiences (SD = .65); 37 reported a mean of 2.5 outpatient experiences (SD = 2.8); and 14 reported a mean of 1.4 intensive outpatient/partial hospitalization experiences (SD = .74). The mean number of total treatment experiences (all settings) was 2.7 (SD = 2.8).

Instruments

Background Questionnaire. This was a questionnaire developed by the authors to gather demographic and descriptive information about the participants. In addition to asking for participant sex, ethnicity, age, and sexual orientation, participants were also asked about time in recovery for alcohol abuse, time in recovery for drug abuse, number and type of treatment experiences (inpatient, outpatient, partial hospital/intensive outpatient), and state of residence.

Affirmative Counselor Behavior Scale-GLB Clients-Client Version (ACBS-GLB-C). The ACBS-GLB-C is an experimental scale adapted from the scale that Matthews et al. (2005) used with addiction counselors. That scale had two subscales that asked addiction counselors to rate the degree to which they engage in specific behaviors with lesbian, gay, and bisexual clients and with all clients. Items were drawn from the literature on affirmative counseling with LGB clients (Matthews et al.). For this study, only the subscale pertaining to behavior with LGB clients was used. The items were rephrased to ask participants, who had been clients, to rate the degree to which their counselors engaged in those specific behaviors. For example, an item from the original scale states, "I help clients establish connections in the gay, lesbian, and bisexual community." In this study the stem was "My counselor . . ." and the item was "helped me establish connections in the gay, lesbian, and bisexual community." A five-point Likert scale was used, with responses ranging from 1 (almost never true) to 5 (almost always true). Additional examples of items include (same stem), "Used language that did not assume I was heterosexual," "Discussed homophobia and heterosexism in my social environment." There are 21 items on the scale. Possible scores range from 21 to 105, with higher scores representing more affirmative behavior.

Participants were asked to complete the scale twice, once for the treatment experience they considered to be most successful and once for the treatment experience they considered to be least successful. If participants had only one treatment experience, they were instructed to complete whichever scale (most or least successful) seemed most appropriate to their situation. All participants who completed only one scale completed it for a "most successful" experience. Matthews et al. (2005) reported an alpha coefficient of .94 for this subscale in the counselor study. The alpha coefficient for this study was .96 for responses pertaining to the counselors in the most successful treatment experience and .93 for those in the least successful experience.

Non-Heterosexist Organizational Climate Scale-Client Version (NHOCS-C). The NHOCS-C is an experimental scale that was originally developed by Bieschke and Matthews (1996) for use with career counselors and was adapted by Matthews et al. (in press) for use with addiction counselors. It measures the degree to which the overall atmosphere in treatment facilities is affirming to lesbian, gay, and bisexual clients. The latter version was used in this study, with some modification to reflect a client respondent rather than a counselor respondent. In addition, four items that contained information such as new employee interview procedures and staff development opportunities that clients would not necessarily know were dropped. The NHOCS contains 15 items that address the climate of the treatment facility. Participants use a five-point Likert scale (1 = not at all true to 5 = completely true) to rate the degree to which each statement is true of the facility they attended. Possible scores range from 15 to 75, with higher scores representing a less heterosexist, more affirming environment. Examples of items are "On the form the program used to collect personal data from new clients, it would have been possible for me to indicate that I was in a same-sex relationship (if this applied to me)," and "Information about local recovery resources for gay, lesbian, and bisexual clients was routinely available (for example gay Alcoholics Anonymous meetings)."

Participants were asked to complete this scale twice, once for the treatment experience they considered to be most successful and once for the treatment experience they considered least successful. If they had only one treatment experience, they were instructed to complete the scale for "most successful" or "least successful" as appropriate. All participants who completed the scale only once completed it as "most successful." Matthews et al. (2005) reported a coefficient alpha of .87 for the NHOCS. The alpha coefficient for the NHOCS-C in this study was .96 for responses for the most successful experience and .85 for responses for the least successful experience.

Procedures

Recruitment announcements were posted, with permission of the list owners, on listservs geared to the lesbian, gay, and bisexual community and/or the addiction recovery community and advertisements were placed in the LGB press. In addition, letters with recruitment flyers were sent to Alcoholics Anonymous groups and to lesbian, gay, and bisexual community centers. Criteria for participation were that an individual self-identify as gay, lesbian, or bisexual, as being in recovery from alcohol and/or drug abuse for at least one year, and as having attended at least one treatment program. Potential participants were instructed to go to a Website that contained a letter of introduction and informed consent. Individuals who chose to participate indicated consent by clicking on a button that said, "I choose to participate." This took them to the survey itself, which was anonymous. When they completed the survey and pressed the "submit" button, participants were taken to a "thank you" page that also gave them an opportunity to request results of the study and/or to be contacted for an interview that would be part of a qualitative follow-up study. The completed surveys and requests for results were sent to separate accounts to insure that the surveys remained anonymous.

RESULTS

To address the first research question, regarding the extent to which lesbian, gay, and bisexual individuals who have been clients report that their addiction counselors and treatment facilities practiced affirmatively, we examined means for individual items and total scores for the ACBS-GLB-C and the NHOCS-C. Means for items on the ACBS-GLB-C ranged from 2.14 to 3.83 for the most successful treatment experience, with 15 of the 21 item means falling below 3.0. For the least successful treatment experience, item means ranged from 1.33 to 2.87, with 13 means falling below 2.0. Scale totals for the ACBS-GLB-C ranged from 21 to 101 for the most successful treatment experience and from 20 to 92 for the least successful treatment experience. Means for items on the NHOCS-C ranged from 1.86 to 3.54 for the most successful treatment experience, with 11 of 15 means falling below 3.0. For the least successful experience, item means ranged from 1.22 to 3.24, with only one mean above 3.0 and 11 means below 2.0. Scale totals for the

NHOCS-C ranged from 15 to 75 for the most successful treatment experience and from 14 to 58 for the least successful experience.

To address the second research question, which asked about differences in scores between experiences considered most successful and those considered least successful, we ran two paired samples t-tests. For the ACBS-GLB-C, there was a significant difference ($t = 3.72$; $df = 30$; $p \leq .001$), with the scores for the most successful treatment experience ($M = 62.26$; $SD = 25.34$) being higher, or more affirmative, than those for the least successful treatment experience ($M = 41.81$; $SD = 17.51$). Another paired samples t-test was run to compare the scores on the NHOCS-C for the most and least successful treatment experiences. The difference between the two was significant ($t = 4.02$; $df = 21$; $p \leq .001$), with the scores for the most successful treatment experience ($M = 43.95$; $SD = 19.38$) being higher, or more affirmative, than those for the least successful treatment experience ($M = 26.55$; $SD = 10.08$).

A series of independent samples t-tests was also run to examine the influence of counselor sexual orientation (lesbian/gay/bisexual or heterosexual) and counselor gender (male or female). For the most successful treatment experience, there were significant differences in mean scores on the ACBS-GLB-C based on both counselor sexual orientation ($t = -5.381$; $df = 45$; $p \leq .001$) and counselor gender ($t = -2.26$; $df = 55$; $p \leq .05$). Mean scores for lesbian/gay/bisexual counselors ($M = 80.00$; $SD = 17.96$) were higher, or more affirmative, than mean scores for heterosexual counselors ($M = 48.23$; $SD = 21.70$). Mean scores for male counselors ($M = 66.28$; $SD = 23.32$) were higher, or more affirmative, than mean scores for female counselors ($M = 52.11$; $SD = 23.31$). For the least successful treatment experience, there were significant differences in mean scores on the ACBS-GLB-C based on counselor gender ($t = -2.73$; $df = 27$; $p \leq .05$). Mean scores for male counselors ($M = 53.36$; $SD = 20.90$) were higher, or more affirmative, than mean scores for female counselors ($M = 34.67$; $SD = 11.42$). A comparison could not be made for counselor sexual orientation because only three participants reported having a counselor who was not heterosexual for their least successful treatment experience.

DISCUSSION

This study sought to examine the extent to which former clients experienced their addiction counselors and treatment facilities as practicing in ways that are affirmative to LGB clients and to examine whether they reported a difference in this between experiences they considered most successful and least successful. The ACBS-GLB-C measures the degree to which counselors engage in behaviors that the professional literature has suggested are indicative of affirmative practice with LGB clients. The NHOCS-C measures the degree to which treatment facilities maintain an environment that is non-heterosexist and affirming of this population. None of the item means on either scale was four or five, which would have suggested more consistently affirmative practice. Indeed, of 21 items on the ACBS-GLB-C, only six item means, less than one third, for the experience reported as most successful and no means for the experience reported as least successful were above 3.0. The remainder of the means for the most successful experience were between 2.0 and 2.99. Thirteen of the means, more than half, for the least successful treatment experience were under 2.0. This suggests that, at best, addiction counselors engage in affirmative behavior with LGB clients only some of the time.

Likewise, for the NHOCS-C, only 4 of 15 item means, less than one third, for the most successful treatment experience and only one item mean for the least successful experience were above 3.0. Eleven item means, more than two thirds, for the least successful treatment experience and one item mean for the most successful experience were lower than 2.0. The low means for the items on the NHOCS-C are particularly troubling given that previous studies (Bieschke & Matthews, 1996; Matthews et al., 2005) have found that a non-heterosexist organizational climate is predictive of counselor affirmative behavior with LGB clients. One of these studies (Matthews et al., 2005) specifically addressed addiction counselors. Thus, not only does a non-heterosexist climate help to create an affirming space in which LGB clients can recover from addiction, but it also seems to influence the degree to which counselors engage in affirmative practice with LGB clients. It seems reasonable to suspect then that absence of such a climate could be detrimental on multiple fronts. The results of this study also suggest that there were differences between the experiences considered most successful and those considered least successful. With both counselor behavior and organizational climate, the experiences clients considered most successful were also the most affirmative.

Additional analyses looked at the potential influence of counselor gender and counselor sexual orientation. There were differences based on counselor sexual orientation for the most successful treatment experience, with LGB counselors being more affirmative than heterosexual counselors. This is consistent with Matthews et al. (2005), who found that one of the factors that predicted addiction counselors' affirmative behavior with LGB clients was counselor sexual orientation. For the least successful treatment experience there were not enough LGB counselors to even do an analysis. There were gender differences for both the most successful and least successful treatment experiences, with male counselors being more affirmative than female counselors. This is contrary to the existing literature, which tends to find female clinicians to be more affirmative than male clinicians (Bieschke, McClanahan, Tozer, Grzegorek, & Park, 2000; Kite & Whitely, 1998). One possible explanation for this may be the intersection of gender and sexual orientation. Scores on the ACBS-GLB-C were significantly higher for LGB counselors than for heterosexual counselors. Two thirds of the LGB counselors for both the most and least successful treatment experiences were male. This has particular ramifications for lesbians who may be looking for role models to address not only sexual orientation but also gender concerns. To whatever extent this study reflects the field, there is a need for treatment facilities to actively recruit more lesbian counselors.

There are limitations to this study. Although the sample was national in scope, it was not a random sample. It was also small. Lesbian, gay, and bisexual individuals in recovery from addiction are a difficult population to reach. They face prejudice and discrimination on multiple levels, so it is often easier to keep one's sexual orientation and one's recovery status hidden. Using an anonymous Internet survey made it possible to reach a small group; however, it is difficult to draw major conclusions based on a sample of 58 participants. In addition, the entire survey was self-report. Thus, the results are based on participants' perceptions of their treatment experiences rather than any objective observation or measurement of what occurred. Still, those perceptions are important and can offer insight into how counselors' and treatment facilities' practices are received. Finally, this was not an outcome study. Determination of most successful and least successful treatment experience was highly subjective. It seems reasonable to suspect that the experiences deemed most successful are those to which they attribute their current sobriety; however, this was not assessed. Likewise, we cannot assume that nothing good came from those experiences deemed least successful. What we can say is that according to participants' subjective reports, there appears to be some association between affirmative practice and more successful results. This is worth studying further in a more controlled manner.

Despite its limitations and exploratory nature, this study does suggest that there is more that addiction counselors and treatment facilities can be doing to address the specific recovery related issues of their LGB clients. This does not necessarily have to mean large expenditures of money or other resources. Much could be accomplished by a proactive effort to increase awareness of the issues facing LGB individuals experiencing addiction and developing the knowledge and skills to address them. It also seems that one avenue for doing this might be to make efforts to hire more openly LGB counselors. The value of this should seem evident in a field that has long recognized the importance of hiring individuals who are themselves in recovery from addiction because of the positive influence they can have as role models.

REFERENCES

Beatty, R. L., Geckle, M. O., Huggins, J., Kapner, C., Lewis, K., Sandstrom, D. J. (1999). Gay men, lesbians, and bisexuals. In B. S. McCrady & E. E. Epstein (Eds.), *Addictions: A comprehensive guidebook* (pp. 542-551). New York: Oxford University Press.

Bieschke., K. J., & Matthews, C. R. (1996). Career counselor attitudes and behaviors with gay, lesbian, and bisexual clients. *Journal of Vocational Behavior, 48*, 243-255.

Bieschke, K. J., McClanahan, M., Tozer, E., Grzegorek, J. L., & Park, J. (2000). Programmatic research on the treatment of lesbian, gay, and bisexual clients: The past, the present, and the course for the future. In R. M. Perez, K. A. DeBord, & K. J. Bieschke (Eds.), *Handbook of counseling and psychotherapy with lesbian, gay, and bisexual clients* (pp. 309-335). Washington, D.C.: American Psychological Association.

Bux, D. A., Jr. (1996). The epidemiology of problem drinking in gay men and lesbians: A critical review. *Clinical Psychology Review, 16*, 277-298.

Cabaj, R. P. (1996). Substance abuse in gay men, lesbians, and bisexuals. In R. P. Cabaj & T. S. Stein (Eds.), *Textbook of homosexuality and mental health* (pp. 783-799). Washington, DC: American Psychiatric Press.

Cabaj, R. P. (1997). Gays, lesbians, and bisexuals. In J. H. Lowinson, P. Ruiz, R. B. Millman, & J. G. Langrod (Eds.), *Substance abuse: A comprehensive textbook* (pp. 725-733). Baltimore, MD: Williams and Wilkins.

Hellman, R. E., Stanton, M., Lee, J., Tytun, A., & Vachon, R. (1989). Treatment of homosexual alcoholics in government-funded agencies: Provider training and attitudes. *Hospital and Community Psychiatry, 40*, 1163-1168.

Israelstam, S. (1986). Alcohol and drug problems of gay males and lesbians: Therapy, counseling, and prevention issues. *The Journal of Drug Issues, 16*, 443-461.

Israelstam, S., & Lambert, S. (1989). Homosexuals who indulge in excessive use of alcohol and drugs: Psychosocial factors to be taken into account by community and intervention workers. *Journal of Alcohol and Drug Education, 34*(3), 54-69.

Kite, M. E., & Whitely, B. B., Jr. (1998). Do heterosexual women and men differ in their attitudes toward homosexuality?: A conceptual and methodological analysis. In G. M. Herek (Ed.), *Psychological perspectives on lesbian and gay issues: Vol 4: Stigma and Sexual Orientation* (pp. 39-61). Thousand Oaks, CA: Sage.

Matthews, C. R., Selvidge, M. M. D., & Fisher, K. (2005). Addiction counselors' attitudes and behaviors toward gay, lesbian, and bisexual clients. *Journal of Counseling and Development, 83*, 57-65.

Paul, J. P., Stall, R., & Bloomfield, K. A. (1991). Gay and alcoholic: Epidemiologic and clinical issues. *Alcohol, Health, and Research World, 15*, 151-160.

Ratner, E. F. (1993). Treatment issues for chemically dependent lesbians, and gay men. In L. D. Garnets & D. C. Kimmel (Eds.), *Psychological perspectives on lesbian and gay male experiences* (pp. 567-578). NY: Columbia University Press.

Schaefer, S., Evans, S., Coleman, E. (1987). Sexual orientation concerns among chemically dependent individuals. *Journal of Chemical Dependency Treatment, 1*, 121-140.

Ubell, V., & Sumberg, D. (1992). Heterosexual therapists treating homosexual addicted clients. *Journal of Chemical Dependency Treatment, 5*, 19-33.

Predicting, Understanding and Changing: Three Research Paradigms Regarding Alcohol Use Among Lesbians

Maria Pettinato

SUMMARY. The author presents a paradigmatic categorization and review of the literature that is available regarding lesbians and alcohol. She illuminates the characteristics, shortcomings, and strengths of Empirical Post Positivist, Interpretive, and Critical Social research paradigms. Results of the various studies are presented while research and funding directions are proposed. *[Article copies available for a fee from The Haworth Document Delivery Service: 1-800-HAWORTH. E-mail address: <docdelivery@haworthpress.com> Website: <http://www.HaworthPress.com> © 2005 by The Haworth Press, Inc. All rights reserved.]*

KEYWORDS. Lesbian, alcohol, paradigm, literature review

Maria Pettinato, RN, PhD, is a faculty member in the College of Nursing at Seattle University teaching undergraduate and graduate pathophysiology. Her research and writing have focused on sexual minority issues including the reduction of violence against lesbian and gay identified youth. She received a NIH-NIDA/National Research Service Award, a Women's Health Nursing Research Training Grant, and a Hester McLaws Nursing Scholarship Award from the University of Washington.

Address correspondence to: Maria Pettinato, 906 E. Boston Street, Seattle, WA 98102 (E-mail: pettinat@seattle.edu).

[Haworth co-indexing entry note]: "Predicting, Understanding and Changing: Three Research Paradigms Regarding Alcohol Use Among Lesbians." Pettinato, Maria. Co-published simultaneously in *Journal of Lesbian Studies* (Harrington Park Press, an imprint of The Haworth Press, Inc.) Vol. 9, No. 3, 2005, pp. 91-101; and: *Making Lesbians Visible in the Substance Use Field* (ed: Elizabeth Ettorre) Harrington Park Press, an imprint of The Haworth Press, Inc., 2005, pp. 91-101. Single or multiple copies of this article are available for a fee from The Haworth Document Delivery Service [1-800-HAWORTH, 9:00 a.m. - 5:00 p.m. (EST). E-mail address: docdelivery@haworthpress.com].

Available online at http://www.haworthpress.com/web/JLS
© 2005 by The Haworth Press, Inc. All rights reserved.
doi:10.1300/J155v09n03_09

In this article, I review the literature on lesbians and alcohol use and in doing so use three predominant research paradigms to characterize this work. Paradigm is defined as, "A way of looking at the world or a perspective on phenomena. . . . The perspective guides research and practice" (Doordan, 1998, p. 91). The three research paradigms I discuss are: *Empirical Post Positivist, Interpretive, and Critical Social*. My assumption is twofold: (1) all paradigms are useful and contribute to the current body of information on lesbians' use of alcohol and (2) these paradigms overlap, providing examples of blurred conceptual boundaries (Jacox, Suppe, Campbell, & Stashinko, 1999).

In the first half of the 20th century, research on lesbians' use of alcohol was predominantly psychoanalytically oriented. Researchers did not differentiate between information obtained from lesbians and gay men (Nardi, 1982). The phenomenon of alcoholism was etiologically linked to homosexuality until the late 1960s when authors of empirical studies began to dispute the homosexuality/alcohol connection (Israelstam & Lambert, 1984). Homosexuality was viewed as a psychiatric disorder (Israelstam & Lambert, 1983, 1986; Nardi, 1982) until it was removed as a diagnosis from the Diagnostic and Statistical Manual (DSM) by the American Psychiatric Association in 1980. Since then, the causal link between homosexuality and alcoholism has been broken. Existing information concerning the use of alcohol among gay men and lesbians, however, remains fraught with discrepancies and challenges unique to studying this population. Additionally, consistent definitions of the term "lesbian" are elusive. In this article, "lesbians" will be defined as biologically female individuals who self identify or behave sexually as homosexual women (IOM, 1999). Some may fall into what may be considered a bisexual identity/behavior category.

EMPIRICAL POST POSITIVIST STUDIES

Empirical Post Positivist researchers ask, "*How can we predict?*" and conduct studies in order to identify common patterns among their participants or subjects. Researchers assume objective, impersonal roles. They use traditional scientific methods with an attempt at controlled experimentation.

> The . . . paradigm focuses on the *discovery* of a reality characterized by patterns and regularities that may be used to describe, explain, and predict phenomena. . . . The Post Positivist emphasizes

the conditions under which certain patterns occur and the need for control over environmental influences to understand the phenomena under study. (Ford-Gilboe, Campbell, & Berman, 1995, p. 16)

While the researcher does not attempt to take an impersonal, observational role of a statistician, she typically holds that an approximate truth already exists and that she is pragmatically attempting to discover it.

Early researchers of lesbians found it extremely challenging to apply such control to recruit and question women who may have been hiding their sexual orientation. The challenge of randomization arose as most of the women in question were leading "closeted" lives. True randomization was impossible as was the ability to control environmental influences. In order to find these women, researchers in the 1970s and '80s went directly to gay/lesbian bars where they knew they would be able to recruit women who identified as lesbian. Ignoring the obvious environmental influences, researchers estimated 30% of lesbians to be abusing alcohol based on their sample from bars. This rate of alcohol abuse was proposed to be three times higher than heterosexual women (Fifield, Latham, & Phillips, 1977; Lewis, Saghir, & Robins, 1982; McKirnan & Peterson, 1989a, 1989b). These skewed results are still commonly referred to today (Council of Scientific Affairs, 1996).

Creating questionable prevalence percentages, the Fifield et. al study (1977) used reported estimate calculations produced by nontraditional statistical manipulations as the basis for their numbers (Bux, 1996), while the Lewis et al. study (1982) recruited lesbians from gay bars and compared their figures to those derived from heterosexual women in a control group not recruited from bars. The McKirnan and Peterson (1989a, 1989b) study began with a hypothesis (negative psychosocial factors in a homosexual sample would produce an increase in alcohol consumption), preconceived deductively by the researchers; they utilized a large survey ($N = 3,400$) as their data source to support their hypothesis.

Two additional studies provide data on lesbian and bisexual women's use of alcohol (Milman & Su, 1973; Saghir & Robins, 1973). Milman and Su (1973) focused on undergraduate women at a mid-Atlantic university. These were mostly socially privileged women obtaining a college education. No data were collected on race or ethnicity. The mean age of the participants in this study was 20.6 years old, the age at which alcohol experimentation during the first extended period away from parental control is common. Saghir and Robins (1973) excluded all non-Caucasian individuals from participating in their research. The mean age of the participants was relatively young at 31. It is valuable for researchers to have knowledge of these earlier studies. However, it is important to consider how the data was obtained, from whom it was obtained, how results were formulated, and who were excluded.

Bloomfield's (1993) data was the first empirical study that did not demonstrate a significant difference in the prevalence rates of alcohol abuse between lesbian and heterosexual women. The heterosexual women sampled had a higher than usual prevalence of "moderate drinking" (18%) than heterosexual women in the general population (7%). In addition, participants were asked to complete a 20 page postal questionnaire, a task that a woman heavily dependent upon alcohol would be unlikely to complete. Thus, it is probable that Bloomfield's sample of lesbians is representative only of moderate to highly functioning individuals. Those finding the performance of basic daily tasks difficult would not have been involved in contributing data.

In 1994, Bradford, Ryan, and Rothblum, and in 1999, Roberts and Sorensen, supported earlier claims that there was a higher rate of "heavy drinking" among lesbians. Bradford et al. (1994) and Skinner and Otis (1996) confirmed the ongoing challenge of randomized subject recruitment. Both emphasized that the hidden nature of the population made it extremely difficult to obtain data that could be considered a representative sample. They maintained that the prevalence of minimal social support, the rejection of lesbians by many organized community institutions, and negative public attitudes toward them continued in the 1990s.

Recently, new information about lesbians' drinking patterns has emerged (Cochran & Mays, 2000; Hughes, 1999; Hughes, Haas, Razzano, Cassidy, & Matthews, 2000). In one urban study that included 63 lesbians, 25% reported abstinence from alcohol over the past 12 months, 46% wondered if at some time in their lives they had a drinking problem, and 17% reported to be in recovery (Hughes, 1999). Cochran and Mays (2000) found that only 7% of lesbian and bisexual women reported heavy alcohol abuse. The psychiatric focus of their research presented two major challenges that may have resulted in the reported low percentage of 'heavy' users: (1) only those who qualified under the strict DSM-IV (1994) classification of Alcohol Dependency Syndrome (ADS) were reported as 'heavy' users and, (2) "lesbian" was defined "behaviorally" so that lesbians who were not sexually active within the past year were excluded.

Hughes et al. (2000) made a concerted effort to reach 55 lesbians within three urban areas. Their sample included women who were non-Caucasian, older, and less than college educated. They found that 21%

of respondents were heavy drinkers and an overwhelming 68% of the non-drinking women reported they were in recovery from alcoholism. Their research supports the hypotheses that abuse of alcohol is a major issue in the lives of lesbians and a disproportionately high number of lesbians are at a heightened risk for ADS as they report drinking more heavily and later into their old age.

Empirical Post Positivist research remains valuable and a challenge methodologically when studying lesbians. As Hughes et al. (2000) demonstrate, there is currently a welcome trend toward reaching women who are more diverse, thus allowing the results to be more generalizable.

INTERPRETIVE STUDIES

Researchers utilizing Interpretive paradigms ask, "*What does it mean?*" A main tenet of Interpretive paradigms is that a researcher values the participants' choice of words, opinions and worldviews. A researcher is like a storyteller (Polkinghorne, 1997); utilizing the Interpretive paradigm, her voice takes on a narrator role. This humanization of the researcher is highly valued, as subjects are viewed as participants and co-actors who contribute to the narrative, not merely those that are observed. The paradigm of Interpretive research is one in which truth is being created as truth is lived.

Interpretive research methodologies include ethnography, phenomenology, grounded theory, and historical research among others (Jacox et al., 1999). Similar to the Post Positivist studies, early Interpretive studies also faced sampling challenges. In 1978, Diamond and Wilsnack conducted a feminist oriented descriptive study in which they questioned 10 lesbian and bisexual college educated women about their experience with alcohol. Like other studies of the time, most women were young and belonged to a privileged social class. Four out of ten reported experiencing symptoms of alcohol dependency and most reported the presence of internalized homophobia.

While Diamond and Wilsnack's (1978) study produced early evidence in support of the existence of internalized homophobia and the role it plays in alcohol abuse, later authors have also theorized about this issue (Bux, 1996; Hall, Stevens, & Meleis, 1994). Hall et al. (1994) supported the significance of the effect of internalized homophobia on lesbians and alcohol abuse. On the other hand, Bux (1996) focused on the lack of empirical evidence to support its influence.

Hall (1990a, 1990b, 1992) conducted a feminist ethnographic study of 35 lesbians in recovery from alcohol addiction. Eventually, her work became one example of the direction that Interpretive studies took as these moved more towards a Critical Social paradigm. The need for societal change as well as a power shift in the recovery field was becoming evident.

A major finding of Hall's (1994a) inquiry was that recovery needs were not consistently met through the traditional 12 step model used by Alcoholics Anonymous (AA; Alcoholics Anonymous World Service, 1976). Her participants reported experiencing AA as an androcentric, paternalistic, authoritarian organization, insensitive to the impact of trauma and family-of-origin issues for women in recovery. They described AA as being rife with sexist language and persistent in the depiction of the "higher power" as a male god (Hall, 1999; Stevens & Hall, 1991, 1992). In contrast, Hellman (1992) supported the 12 step model for lesbians who are dual diagnosed individuals.

Highlighting the link between childhood sexual abuse (CSA) and alcoholism, Hall published an additional secondary analysis of her 1992 study in 1996. Since CSA is a common phenomenon among heterosexual women who abuse alcohol, it was not surprising to find it prominent among lesbians. McNally and Finnegan (1992) created a five stage developmental model after interviewing eight lesbian and bisexual women. They proposed a powerful dynamic operating between sexual identity and alcoholism and five developmental stages: beginning; drinking; recovering alcoholic; lesbian; and ongoing management stages.

Rothberg and Kidder (1992) suggested specific therapeutic interventions to be used with lesbians who abuse alcohol and are adult children of alcoholics (ACOAs). The interventions include mechanisms that help each ACOA to learn about her family and her role in it and to know she is not alone, to come out, and to be guided through stages from denial to acceptance. Reyes (1998) conducted an ethnographic study with Latina lesbian and bisexual women, the first to focus on an ethnic minority population of lesbian and bisexual substance users. She emphasized that the 12 step model used in AA was disempowering. She echoed the sentiments of earlier authors regarding the need to go beyond AA's 12 step model (Deevey & Wall, 1992; Hall, 1990a, 1990b, 1992; Heyward, 1992). Reyes' (1998) research is another example of a project that began within the Interpretive paradigm and moved toward a Critical Social one.

Finally, Parks (1999a, 1999b) utilized phenomenological methods to question lesbians who identified as "social drinkers" and reported that they drank alcohol while exploring and immersing themselves within the lesbian subculture. Alcohol consumption was not only a focus at gay/lesbian bars, but also was dominant in other domains of the subculture such as sports leagues and lesbian social networks.

CRITICAL SOCIAL PARADIGM

Researchers using a Critical Social approach ask, "*Who is in power and how can power dynamics be changed?*" This Critical Social research paradigm addresses how sociopolitical and cultural factors influence the experience of research participants (Jacox et al., 1999). Interventions emanating from this paradigm focus on system changes as well as individual empowerment. Participatory action, or praxis, is expected from both researchers and participants. Truth or reality is viewed as an evolving concept, created or co-constructed by participants and researchers. In this context, Ford-Gilboe et al. (1995) wrote:

> The aim of research within the Critical paradigm is the development of approaches that have the potential to expose hidden power imbalances . . . to empower those involved to understand . . . to transform, the world. . . . Implicit . . . is the idea as people learn to perceive social and political contradictions, they become able to take action against oppressive structures in their lives. (p. 17)

Hall (1990a) evidenced use of a Critical paradigm by stating that "western norms are androcentric, and against such standards, women are assigned an abnormal status" (p. 94). She noted that lesbians are not viewed as real or normal women by many in western societies and lesbian alcoholics are more marginalized. Hall (1994b) also focused on the negative health care experiences of lesbians recovering from alcohol abuse and how these created an oppressive environment. Participants offered accounts of health care providers who changed demeanor following disclosure of their patient's sexual orientation. She called for an overall societal/environmental change and highlighted the need for a more welcoming therapeutic environment for lesbians in recovery. Along with Hall's (1992) critical discussions of the AA disease model, other authors have shown the need for change in the therapeutic milieu of lesbians (Amico, 2003; Deevey & Wall, 1992; Heyward, 1992).

Deevey and Wall (1992) and Heyward (1992) identified themselves as lesbian alcoholics in recovery and criticized the 12 step model. In a theoretical paper, Deevey and Wall (1992) replaced the 12 step model with their own ideas on treating lesbians. Heyward (1992) focused on the contributing factor of internalized homophobia. Amico (2003) concurs with the aforementioned lesbian authors in recovery and supports the use of "alternative spiritualities," especially for those that perceive themselves as having been "spiritually abused" by those misusing the concepts of 12 step programs (p. 18).

CONCLUSIONS

This article provides a useful means of categorizing the research on lesbian and alcohol use in a systematic way, according to three main research paradigms. In spite of the influence of the mass media and the notion that it may be 'chic' to be a lesbian for some urban teenagers, (Latimer, 1996) many lesbians remain "closeted" and possess varying levels of internalized homophobia. They experience the same social stigmatization and prejudice experienced by lesbians of earlier decades. Little or no research was found that particularly investigated the alcohol use experiences of those lesbians who are midlife or older, have less formal education, live in non-urban areas, and/or who belong to an ethnic minority. This lack of research among these sub-groups of lesbians results in a significant level of invisibility.

The 1999 report of the Institute of Medicine's Committee on Lesbian Health Research affirmed that although an emphasis on women's health research was evident in the 1990s, there has been little funding for research on lesbian health. Roberts (2001) reported that lesbian and bisexual women's health has since emerged as an area of study. While it may be an emerging research area, it does not have funding priority. Funded research on lesbian and bisexual women continues to lag behind research involving the general population of women (Hughes et al., 2000). As researchers compete for available funding, time and energy may be wasted if the battle for funding is waged with each other. In this competition, all paradigms should be represented. Furthermore, utilizing and respecting all paradigms is one way research on minority populations will move forward in a timely fashion. Future research agendas and funding priorities should include all paradigms. We should recognize the value in asking, How can we predict?, How can we understand? and How can we change? in the lesbian and alcohol field.

REFERENCES

Alcoholics Anonymous World Services. (1976). *Twelve steps and twelve traditions.* New York: Author.

American Psychiatric Association. (1980). *Diagnostic and statistical manual of mental disorders* (3rd ed.). Washington, DC: Author.

American Psychiatric Association. (1994). *Diagnostic and statistical manual of mental disorders* (4th ed.). Washington, DC: Author.

Amico, J. M. (2003). Healing from 'spiritual abuse': Assisting gay and lesbian clients. *Addiction Professional 1*(5), 18-20.

Bloomfield, K. (1993). A comparison of alcohol consumption between lesbians and heterosexual women in an urban population. *Drug and Alcohol Dependence, 33*, 257-269.

Bradford, J., Ryan, C., & Rothblum, E. D. (1994). National lesbian health care survey: Implications for mental health care. *Journal of Consulting & Clinical Psychology, 62*(2),228-242.

Bux, D. A. (1996). The epidemiology of problem drinking in gay men and lesbians: A critical review. *Clinical Psychology Review, 16*(4), 277-298.

Cochran, S. D., & Mays, V. M. (2000). Relation between psychiatric syndromes and behaviorally defined sexual orientation in a sample of the US population. *American Journal of Epidemiology, 151*(5), 516-523.

Council on Scientific Affairs (1996). Health care needs of gay men and lesbians in the United States. *The Journal of the American Medical Association, 275*(17), 1354-1359.

Deevey, S., & Wall, L. J. (1992). How do lesbian women develop serenity? *Health Care for Women International, 13*, 199-208.

Diamond, D. L., & Wilsnack, S. C. (1978). Alcohol use among lesbians: A descriptive study. *Journal of Homosexuality, 4*(2), 123-142.

Doordan, A. M. (1998). *Research survival guide.* New York: Lippincott.

Fifield, L., Latham, J., & Phillips, C. (1977). *Alcoholism in the gay community: The price of alienation, isolation, and oppression.* Los Angeles: Gay Community Center.

Ford-Gilboe, M., Campbell, J., & Berman, H. (1995). Stories and numbers: Coexistence without compromise. *Advances in Nursing Science, 18*(1), 14-26.

Hall, J. M. (1990a). Alcoholism in lesbians: Developmental, symbolic interactionist, and critical perspectives. *Health Care for Women International, 11*, 89-107.

Hall, J. M. (1990b). Alcoholism recovery in lesbian women: A theory in development. *Scholarly Inquiry for Nursing Practice: An International Journal, 4*(2), 109-125.

Hall, J. M. (1992). An exploration of lesbians' images of recovery from alcohol problems. *Health Care for Women International, 13*, 181-198.

Hall, J. M. (1994a). The experiences of lesbians in alcoholics anonymous. *Western Journal of Nursing Research, 16*(5), 556-576.

Hall, J. M. (1994b). Lesbians recovering from alcohol problems: An ethnographic study of health care experiences. *Nursing Research, 43*(4), 238-244.

Hall, J. M. (1996). Pervasive effects of childhood sexual abuse in lesbians' recovery from alcohol problems. *Substance Use & Misuse, 31*(2), 225-239.

Hall, J. M. (1999). Marginalization revisited: Critical, postmodern, and liberation perspectives. *Advances in Nursing Science*, 22(2), p.88-102.
Hall, J. M., Stevens, P. E., & Meleis, A. I. (1994). Marginalization: A guiding concept for valuing diversity in nursing knowledge development. *Advances in Nursing Science*, 16(4), 23-41.
Hellman, R. E. (1992). Dual diagnosis issues with homosexual persons. *Journal of Chemical Dependency*, 5(1), 105-117.
Heyward, C. (1992). Healing addiction and homophobia: Reflections on empowerment and liberation. *Journal of Chemical Dependency Treatment*, 5(1), 5-18.
Hughes, T. L. (1999). *Sexual identity and alcohol use: A comparison of lesbians' and heterosexual women's patterns of drinking*. Paper presented at "New Approaches to Research on Sexual Orientation, Mental Health and Substance Abuse," Baltimore, MD.
Hughes, T. L., Haas, A. P., Razzano, L., Cassidy, R., & Matthews, A. K. (2000). Comparing lesbians' and heterosexual women's mental health: Findings from a multi-site study. *Journal of Gay & Lesbian Social Services*, 11(1), 57-76.
Institute of Medicine (IOM). (1999). *Lesbian health: Current assessment and directions for the future*. Washington, DC: National Academy Press.
Israelstam, S., & Lambert, S. (1983). Homosexuality as a cause of alcoholism: A historical perspective. *International Journal of Addiction*, 18, 1085-1107.
Israelstam, S., & Lambert, S. (1984). Gay bars. *Journal of Drug Issues*, 14, 637-653.
Israelstam, S., & Lambert, S. (1986). Homosexuality and alcohol: Observation and research after the psychoanalytic era. *The International Journal of the Addictions*, 21, (4 & 5), 509-537.
Jacox, A., Suppe, F., Campbell, J. & Stashinko, E. (1999). Diversity in philosophical approaches. In A. S. Hinshaw, S. L. Feetham, & J. L. F. Shaver, Eds. *Handbook of Clinical Nursing Research*, (pp. 3-15). Thousand Oaks: Sage.
Latimer, J. (1996). Lesbian chic goes to Hollywood: But will the affair with women continue? *Herizons*, 10(2), 24-5, 27.
Lewis, C. E., Saghir, M.T., & Robins, E. (1982). Drinking patterns in homosexual and heterosexual women. *Journal of Clinical Psychiatry*, 43, 277-279.
McKirnan, D. J., & Peterson, P. L. (1989a). Alcohol and drug use among homosexual men and women: Epidemiology and population characteristics. *Addictive Behaviors*, 14, 545-553.
McKirnan, D. J., & Peterson, P. L. (1989b). Psychosocial and cultural factors in alcohol and drug abuse: An analysis of a homosexual community. *Addictive Behaviors*, 14, 555-563.
McNally, E. B., & Finnegan, D. G. (1992), Lesbian recovering alcoholics: A qualitative study of identity transformation. *Journal of Chemical Dependency Treatment*, 5(1), 93-103.
Milman, D. H. & Su, W. H. (1973). Patterns of drug usage among university students: V. heavy use of marihuana and alcohol by undergraduates. *Journal of the American College Health Association*, 21, 181-187.
Nardi, P. (1982). Alcoholism and homosexuality: A theoretical perspective. *Journal of Homosexuality*, 7, 9-25.
Parks, C. (1999a). Lesbian identity development: An examination of difference across generations. *American Journal of Orthopsychiatry*, 69(3), 347-361.

Parks, C. (1999b). Bicultural competence: A mediating factor affecting alcohol use practices and problems among lesbian social drinkers. *Journal of Drug Issues, 29*(1), 135-153.

Polkinghorne, D. E. (1997). Reporting qualitative research as practice. In W. G. Tierney & Y. S. Lincoln (Eds.), *Representation and the text: Re-framing the narrative voice* (pp. 8, 10). Albany: State University of New York Press.

Reyes, M. (1998). Latina lesbian and alcohol and other drug: Social work implications.*Alcoholism Treatment Quarterly, 16*(1-2), 179-192.

Roberts, S. J. (2001). Lesbian health research: A review and recommendations for future Research. *Health Care for Women International, 22,* (537-552).

Roberts, S. J., & Sorensen, L. (1999). Health related behaviors and cancer screening of lesbians: Results from the Boston lesbian health project. *Women & Health, 28*(4), 1-12.

Rothberg, B. P., & Kidder, D. M. (1992). Double trouble: Lesbians emerging from alcoholic families. *Journal of Chemical Dependency Treatment, 5*(1), 77-92.

Saghir, M. T., & Robins, E. (1973). *Male and female homosexuality: A comprehensive investigation.* Baltimore, MD: Williams and Wilkins.

Skinner, W. F., & Otis, M. D. (1996). Drug and alcohol use among lesbian and gay people in a southern U.S. sample: Epidemiological, comparative, and methodological finding from the Trilogy Project. *Journal of Homosexuality, 30*(3), 59-92.

Stevens, P. E. & Hall, J. (1991). A critical historical analysis of the medical construction of lesbianism. *International Journal of Health Services, 21*(2), 291-307.

Stevens, P. E. & Hall, J. (1992). Applying critical theories to nursing in communities. *Public Health Nursing, 9* (1), 2-9.

Exploring an HIV Paradox: An Ethnography of Sexual Minority Women Injectors

Rebecca M. Young
Samuel R. Friedman
Patricia Case

SUMMARY. HIV risk and infection are markedly increased among sexual minority women injectors compared to other injecting drug users. Our ethnographic exploration of this well-documented but poorly under-

---

Rebecca M. Young, PhD, is Assistant Professor of Women's Studies at Barnard College. Samuel R. Friedman, PhD, is a Senior Research Fellow and Director of the Social Theory Core at the Center for Drug Use and HIV Research of National Development and Research Institutes. Patricia Case, ScD, is a lecturer in the Department of Social Medicine at Harvard Medical School.

Address correspondence to: Rebecca M. Young, Barnard College, Department of Women's Studies, 3009 Broadway, 201 Barnard Hall, New York, NY 10027 (E-mail: ryoung@barnard.edu).

The authors extend deep gratitude to the many women who shared their life stories and spaces with them as they conducted this study, and to the entire research team: Marysol Asencio, Michael Clatts, Toni Gallo, Amber Hollibaugh, Susan Keyes, Brenda Roche, and Rebecca Sumner-Burgos.

Initial research for this project was supported by NIDA grant R01 DA10870-01 (Samuel R. Friedman, Principal Investigator). Continuing analyses were supported by NIDA grant R03 DA14399-01 (Rebecca M. Young, Principal Investigator).

[Haworth co-indexing entry note]: "Exploring an HIV Paradox: An Ethnography of Sexual Minority Women Injectors." Young, Rebecca M., Samuel R. Friedman, and Patricia Case. Co-published simultaneously in *Journal of Lesbian Studies* (Harrington Park Press, an imprint of The Haworth Press, Inc.) Vol. 9, No. 3, 2005, pp. 103-116; and: *Making Lesbians Visible in the Substance Use Field* (ed: Elizabeth Ettorre) Harrington Park Press, an imprint of The Haworth Press, Inc., 2005, pp. 103-116. Single or multiple copies of this article are available for a fee from The Haworth Document Delivery Service [1-800-HAWORTH, 9:00 a.m. - 5:00 p.m. (EST). E-mail address: docdelivery@haworthpress.com].

Available online at http://www.haworthpress.com/web/JLS
© 2005 by The Haworth Press, Inc. All rights reserved.
doi:10.1300/J155v09n03_10

stood phenomenon included 270 interviews and over 350 field observations with 65 sexual minority women injectors in New York City and Boston. We discuss findings in relation to four preliminary hypotheses. Neither the presence of gay or bisexual men in risk networks, nor a sense of invulnerability due to lesbian (or other sexual minority) identity seem to be plausible explanations of increased HIV among sexual minority women injectors. However, multiple marginalization was found to be pervasive and to have severe consequences that can be traced to increased HIV risk for many women in the study. *[Article copies available for a fee from The Haworth Document Delivery Service: 1-800-HAWORTH. E-mail address: <docdelivery@haworthpress.com> Website: <http://www.HaworthPress.com> © 2005 by The Haworth Press, Inc. All rights reserved.]*

KEYWORDS. Women and HIV, injection, intersectionality, drug use, lesbian, bisexual

THE HIV PARADOX

What is it about being a sexual minority woman that increases the risks associated with being an injecting drug user? More than 20 large epidemiological studies have consistently found higher HIV risk, incidence, and prevalence among injecting drug users who are lesbian, gay, bisexual, or other women who have sex with women compared to other injecting drug users, even when other risks (e.g., sex work, history of incarceration, drug of choice) are controlled (Ompad et al., 2003; Young, Friedman, Case, Asencio, & Clatts, 2000). Sexual minority women are more than five times as likely as other injectors (male and female) to seroconvert (Friedman, Jose, Deren, Des Jarlais, Neaigus, 1995), and more than twice as likely to be HIV-infected as other injectors (relevant studies are summarized in Young et al., 2000).

A brief note on terms is in order. Same-sex sexual behavior and minority sexual identity do not perfectly overlap, and both same-sex behavior and minority sexual identity have been associated with increased HIV risks among women injectors. In the past, we have advocated for the term "women who have sex with women (WSW)" as the most inclusive referent for this group, approaching WSW as a status rather than a behavioral marker per se (Young et al., 2000). Here, we use the term "sexual minority women" to more clearly reflect that HIV patterns alone suggest that same-sex behavior, while different from identity, is more than "just" behavior. Since woman to woman sexual transmission of HIV occurs only rarely (Kennedy, Scarlett, Duerr & Chu, 1995), it cannot account for increased risk among sexual minority women relative to other injectors. Yet no other behaviors or experiences examined in epidemiological studies to date can fully explain their heightened vulnerability to HIV.

Coming to grips with this long-standing paradox is critical. There are an estimated 100,000 or more sexual minority women injectors in the U.S. alone (Young et al., 2000), yet without a clear articulation of the mechanisms that increase their HIV risk, interventions for this large group are difficult to conceive. Further, as both sexual minorities and injecting drug users, this group is doubly marginalized. Tracing the specific ways that HIV risk becomes elevated for these women, many of whom are also poor and of color, can provide insights into how intersecting marginalities operate in the arena of health.

To explore this well-documented but poorly understood phenomenon, we conducted a targeted ethnographic study of sexual minority women injectors in New York City and Boston from 1997 through 2000. Our broad aims were to describe the lives and social environments, including but not limited to the drug-related and sexual risk behaviors and networks, of a broad range of women injecting drug users who have sex with women.

PRELIMINARY HYPOTHESES

We began with four preliminary hypotheses: (1) *Networks*–Lesbian or bisexual women drug users in some studies were more likely than other women drug users to have sex with and/or inject drugs with gay or bisexual men (Friedman, Curtis, Neaigus, Jose, & Des Jarlais, 1999), who are themselves more likely than other men to be HIV seropositive; (2) *The myth of lesbian invulnerability*–Community activists and lesbian organizers have suggested that lesbians may be particularly unlikely to take risk reduction measures because of a sense that "lesbians don't get AIDS" (Hollibaugh, 1994; Reyes, 1991); (3) *Lack of information*–Since few HIV prevention materials specifically address sexual minority women injectors, this group might be uninformed about basic HIV prevention strategies for safer sex and injection; (4) *Multiple marginalization*–Research on discrimination and health (Krieger, 2001), as well as theories of intersectionality (Crenshaw, 1995), suggest that

METHODS

Fieldwork comprised three stages over 40 months. Stage I involved ethnographic mapping (Clatts, Davis, & Atillasoy, 1995) of the New York project areas to identify injection settings and social spaces where sexual minority women injectors spend time. We conducted key informant interviews with other injectors who have regular contact with sexual minority women, patrons and staff of establishments in the ethnography areas, and 50 key personnel of 33 local agencies (e.g., needle exchanges, drug treatment, and LGBT community agencies). Stage II was an ethnography of sexual minority women injectors in East Harlem and the Lower East Side, recruited via targeted sampling from street settings and referral by other participants. A brief screening determined eligibility on three criteria: (1) female gender; (2) injecting drug use within the past 12 months; and (3) any history of sex (self-defined) with a woman. We conducted 270 open-ended Life History interviews with 65 sexual minority women injectors and 33 interviews with 23 "interactors" defined as sexual partners of sexual minority women injectors, or sexual minority women with a past history of injecting. Each 1-2 hour interview, conducted in English and/or Spanish, was taped and transcribed verbatim. Spanish interviews were translated to English for analysis. We also recorded 350 ethnographic observations, including over 70 injection episodes. Stage III was a small comparison ethnography in Boston, similar to that described for New York. Fieldwork in both New York and Boston continued through December 1999.

Ongoing, iterative analysis began during fieldwork and consisted of a running description of the sample and their HIV-related risk behaviors, reflections on the preliminary hypotheses, thematic analysis of the life history interviews, and formation of emergent hypotheses. Because our administrative offices were located in the World Trade Center, our original data and project files were destroyed on September 11, 2001. An interim dataset from the data-cleaning phase was available from off-site storage. However, all administrative memos tracking the data cleaning process, and all tapes which could be used to re-clean raw transcripts, were destroyed. A painstaking reconstruction process involved reconciling the interim dataset with other material that survived, such as

heightened HIV risks and rates may be the result of multiple, intersecting forms of marginalization due to status as women, sexual minorities, illicit drug users, and, for many, as women of color and poor people.

coding memos that contained cleaned segments of interviews. For this paper, we explored four preliminary hypotheses, using Atlas.ti to examine reconstructed field observations and interview transcripts.

Before examining findings related to the hypotheses, we describe demographic and sexual characteristics of the sample.

CHARACTERISTICS OF THE SAMPLE

Demographics. Women in this sample are demographically similar to other local samples of women injectors, and dramatically *unlike* others usually represented in the lesbian health literature. Two-thirds are ethnic minorities, 34% Latina, including Puerto Rican (26%), Dominican (7%) and other (1%); 34% non-Latina white; 23% African American; 9% Native American, Asian, multiracial, or "other." The vast majority have a high-school degree or less. About 20% reported some college education. Their ages range from 19 to 53 years, with a mean of 35. A majority of the respondents are mothers.

At the initial interview, more than half the sample considered themselves homeless. Respondents' diverse socioeconomic positions are reflected by the range of their living situations, which included public housing projects, illegally subdivided private apartments, and "squats" such as a tent in a community garden and a hollow space inside the support beam of an overpass. At the other extreme, a few lived in secure luxury apartments.

Sexual Identity and Relationships. Contrary to the assumption that same-sex involvement among women drug users is mostly "situational" (e.g., Sterk, 1999), the majority of respondents preferred women both sexually and as relational partners. In the screening interview, most identified as gay/lesbian (n = 33; 50.7%) or bisexual (n = 15; 23%); with fewer identifying as straight or heterosexual (n = 14; 21.5%), or refusing sexual identity labels (n = 3; 4.6%). The life history interviews and ethnographic interactions, however, showed that women's preferred terms are shifting and contextual, e.g., three women who initially identified as heterosexual, and one woman who rejected all identity terms, later called themselves bisexual; several women who identified as bisexual at screening later called themselves gay or lesbian. Flexible use of sexual identity terms means that single labels are sometimes misleading. Gabi, for example, a 40-year-old mother of six, generally describes herself as lesbian, but once explained that "I was bisexual for like, I think, 17 years. And out of those 17 years, these last ten years I've been strictly gay." In spite of their minority sexual identities, respondents had almost no connection to formal LGBT organizations or services, although most occasionally attend lesbian bars or events such as Gay Pride celebrations.

While all respondents had had sex with at least one woman, almost all had also had sex with men. About three-quarters of respondents are or have been in committed relationships with other women, and about a third of respondents are or have been in committed relationships (including marriage) with men; these groups heavily overlap.

Drug Use and Injection-Related Risks. Most women in this sample are active, daily injectors who prefer heroin, a heroin-cocaine combination, or other opiates as their primary drug. In observations of injection events, we saw the same range of risky injection and risk reduction practices that have been reported for other injectors (e.g., Jose et al., 1993; see discussion of the second and third hypotheses, below, for more information on injection risk).

Predictably, respondents with more economic and class privilege tended to be buffered from the risks of violence and arrest associated with drug use, because these women frequently paid intermediaries to purchase their drugs and injection equipment. On the one hand, this meant that the direct price of drugs was somewhat higher, but the long term "real price" in terms of avoiding violence and criminal justice involvement is no doubt lower. On the other hand, the most economically and socially disenfranchised women were the most likely to freely use needle exchanges and other services that identify clients as drug users.

REVISITING THE HYPOTHESES

Networks. Our first hypothesis was that increased HIV risk among sexual minority women injectors could be explained rather simply by the presence of gay and/or bisexual men in their risk networks (at presumably higher rates than would be found for other women injectors). In fact, we observed or heard about very little sharing of injection equipment or sexual contact between sexual minority women and men injectors in this study. We also observed fairly limited *social* contact with gay, bisexual, or other men who have sex with men. Multiple life history interviews, however, suggested that there was much more contact between sexual minority women and men (including gay and bisexual male injectors) prior to the 1990s. Interestingly, this was true among respondents of all ethnic and socioeconomic groups. Several of the older

African American women remembered specific drug spots in Harlem where Black lesbian and gay drug users would hang out and get high together during the 1970s and early 1980s. The older white respondents reported similar lesbian and gay drug scenes, whether they had been in exclusive private schools or in squats on the Lower East Side (or both):

> Yeah. I slept with a lot of guys who were either identified as bisexual or had had experiences with men. In the '80s, it was sort of de rigueur [for males] to have . . . had at least one experience with a guy even if you found it unpleasant.

Thus, while our ethnographic data don't directly support the hypothesis, it is possible that at least some of the increased HIV rates observed among sexual minority women injectors is the residual effect of greater mixing between sexual minority men and women injectors during the early stages of the epidemic.

Lesbian Invulnerability Myth. The data also fail to support our second hypothesis, the idea that (mis)identification of lesbians as a "low-risk group" may lead some sexual minority women injectors to discount their HIV risks, possibly even risks associated with injection or sex with men (Young, Weissman, & Cohen, 1992; Reyes, 1991). In contrast to this hypothesis, most respondents (including those who identify as lesbian) expressed a strong sense of vulnerability to HIV, with those who have tested negative characterizing their seronegative status as "miraculous," "shocking," and "lucky." As Lorna says, "I say it's a miracle that I haven't got it because I didn't use condoms, didn't wash out works. Didn't do any of that."

Most women reported using condoms for sex with men most of the time. Olive's comments were typical: "I would not fuck a man and not have a rubber. I'm a hardcore lesbian but I have . . . I always carry a condom in my wallet." Certainly, many women in this sample had difficulties practicing safer sex with male partners, and practicing safe injection, as do other women injectors. But the language that sexual minority women in this study used to refer to condom use is different from what is usually reported for women, in that it is active, and there is little emphasis on male resistance to condoms. Rather than saying their male partners do or don't use condoms, these women say "I use condoms" or "I didn't use condoms"; when they describe difficulties using condoms, they tend to describe their own resistance or inertia, rather than partners' resistance. Carlotta, one of the few women who reported sex with a bisexual man, mused over how she has managed to remain uninfected:

I don't know cause I never used condoms even when I was having sex [with him]. And I just, it's lucky, I guess. Like I said it could be laying in my system and it's just not surfacing yet. But, um, every time I took the test it came back negative . . . but I don't never jump for joy.

Most women also had experience using barriers for giving or receiving oral-vulval or oral-anal sex, and reported using dental dams, "sex dams" (such as Glide Dams), and plastic wrap. However, women generally reported a strong dislike of barriers for sex with women, saying they are "no fucking good" and "defeat the purpose of sex." Very few women consistently used them, even with their HIV-positive partners. For example, Jan, whose lover is HIV infected, describes why she doesn't use barriers: "There's no sexual personality, you're covering it up, you can't see it, you can't feel it, you can't taste it."

Women we interviewed did not claim to always do safer sex or injection, but they are not oblivious to their HIV risks. Sexual minority women injectors in this study take their HIV risks seriously, and feel personally responsible for the risks that they do or don't take. While some lesbian injectors may feel protected from HIV by their lesbianism, we are confident that a sense of invulnerability to HIV is not a significant factor in the increased HIV risk among sexual minority women injectors.

Lack of Information. Sexual minority women injectors we interviewed did not lack basic HIV transmission and prevention information. While we found some confusion regarding the level of risk associated with woman-to-woman sex, this mirrors the sparse data about woman-to-woman sexual transmission, including the lack of risk probabilities for specific sexual acts (Young, 1994). When we probed the idea that "lesbians are at lower risk," we found that respondents universally associated this idea with sex between women, while sharing injection equipment and unprotected sex with men were consistently recognized as risk behaviors. Sugar, who has done street outreach for a needle exchange program and is well-versed on what she calls the "official safe sex party line," expresses this distinction when she says: "And that's funny, because I will not fuck a man without a condom. But I've never fucked a woman with any protection. [Laugh]"

Importantly, respondents understood that sexual transmission of HIV between women is possible (and has been documented, e.g., Kwakwa, 2003), though it is more difficult than sexual transmission between either two men or a man and a woman. Moreover, most women reported some safer sex practice, such as avoiding oral sex during menstruation, or using precautions such as condoms for sex toys. Sexual minority women's failure to use barriers with women partners does not seem to reflect ignorance, then, but a "considered risk."

Multiple Marginalization. In contrast to our other hypotheses, the notion that sexual minority women injectors are subject to multiple forms of marginalization that increase overall HIV risk was strongly supported by this study. Sexual minority women injectors are systematically subjected to poor treatment in a wide range of formal and informal institutions, and this can be traced to increased HIV risk.

Their low status within networks of injectors is a case in point. Other injectors often stigmatize sexual minority women as dykes, "aggressors," or lesbians, and this affects the extent to which sexual minority women benefit from in-network resource exchanges. For example, it is routine for injectors to share extra clean syringes that they have obtained from needle exchange, or to provide them at very low cost. We observed sexual minority women to have difficulties with such "secondary exchange": they were refused, made to pay (when others were given syringes for free), and/or made to pay higher prices than non-sexual minority injectors. In one incident in a park bathroom, we observed a lesbian injector being refused a clean syringe by a woman who said she didn't have any to spare. When the lesbian left the bathroom, the other woman made a derogatory remark about "that dyke," and proceeded to provide a (free) clean syringe to a third woman. This incident is notable in part because, like much discrimination, it went on behind the back of the stigmatized person, who remained unaware that she had been the target of discrimination.

Network membership *per se* does not govern such exchanges, since exchange refusals of this sort happened between women who would be considered "connected" in terms of knowing one another. Neither the size of networks, nor tracing the number of exchanges will necessarily reveal these dynamics, especially when requests are not outright denied, but are met with higher prices. In the long run, higher prices also translate into increased risks, as sexual minority women may need to undertake more "hustles" to pay for their needs.

A recent study of HIV-positive women found that sexual minority women report significantly greater support from friends and groups or organizations than do heterosexual women (Cooperman, Simoni, and Lockhart, 2003). In partial agreement with that study, women in this sample tend to have very intimate and mutually supportive networks with other sexual minority women injectors, but they had little to no supportive contact with organizations or formal groups. Literally none of our respondents were members of LGBT organizations, churches, or other social groups. Both New York City and Boston had Lesbian AIDS Projects during the time of our fieldwork, but with only two exceptions, our respondents were not connected to those projects, either. The women in this study were also poorly served by organizations serving drug users, as those agencies mostly thought that "lesbian" issues should be handled by LGBT groups. LGBT organizations, in turn, tended to regard these sexual minority women injectors as "not real lesbians" or "not really gay," confirming Hollibaugh's (1994) point that race, class, and cultural biases fuel lesbian communities' inability to mount an effective and supportive response to HIV/AIDS.

This double outsider status is apparent in women's descriptions of their interactions with medical providers. On the one hand, mainstream medical providers, especially those who primarily serve poor women and/or drug users, used overt hostility and derogatory language, especially in regard to women's sexual minority status. Gabi's account of the questions doctors asked her in prison exemplifies this:

> You know, the doctors in prison, they, they, you know, they ask you all kind of shit. 'Oh, you ain't been with men? I can't believe it. You're gay? You mean to tell me no dicks? After you've taken so much dick?' Cause that's the way they say it.

On the other hand, sexual minority women injectors described less hostility from medical providers in LGBT settings, but they also described subtle ways in which they were made to feel like they did not belong in these settings. Sandy's account of the questions she gets from clinicians at an LGBT clinic shows the mistrust that women frequently encountered:

> It's the whole thing, 'Are you pregnant? Do you use protection? Are you pregnant?' No. I'm not pregnant. And they're like, 'Are you positive you're not pregnant?' I'm like, yes. And that's when I say, yes, because I'm gay. I'm a lesbian. I don't go out with men. Or if they say, how can you be sexually active and not use a condom? Or something like that. And I'll be like, no, I'm a lesbian. But it happens all the time.

Several respondents shared their frustration at having to constantly reiterate their status as lesbians, even when they specifically go to

LGBT venues in order to be accepted. A significant minority of women did describe lesbian-friendly environments in some harm reduction programs (including needle exchange, and some methadone programs). This was usually limited to information about safer sex with women. For example, Renee was "really impressed" with a "women's health program" that helped women drug users to talk about physical and sexual abuse. However, she said the program was "totally hetero-based," and had no information for women who were abused by their female partners (a situation that some women in this study had experienced), commenting, "I took offence to it because, again, that's like a slap in the face. You know? Something's wrong with me!"

While they are marginalized by others, sexual minority women injectors do have rich and highly connected networks among themselves, but this may be a double edged sword: dense networks among injectors have been associated in other research with high HIV infection and levels of risk behavior (Friedman et al. 1999), and "very close" relationships are often sites of riskier behavior, such as receptive syringe sharing (Neaigus, Freidman, Kottiri, & Des Jarlais, 2001). Compared to other ethnographic descriptions of women drug users' relationships in the literature (Maher, 1997; Sterk, 1999), sexual minority women injectors in this study described their relationships in ways that denoted a high degree of intimacy. A striking limitation of these connections is that they almost never crossed class lines, though networks and intimate relationships often did include women of various ethnicities.

Finally, key institutions, such as shelters, drug treatment programs, and the criminal justice system often stigmatize sexual minority women as "sexually inappropriate" regardless of actual behavior, and subject them to intensified surveillance and sanctions (Young, 2003). This "sexual profiling" was much more pervasive in the lives of the poor women in this study, as women with more resources were less frequently subject to intense bureaucratic scrutiny. Ramona, a middle-aged woman in Boston, described problems staying in shelters:

> [T]hey don't like the relationship that me and her is in. . . . They don't like gay women. . . . But if she's with a man, it's OK. They'll accept it. . . . So far what's been happening–the staff are the one that say they don't like the fact of us both being there and they felt, well, maybe I should go to another shelter.

Women identified by staff as lesbians were not allowed the same sort of physical contact that other women enjoyed and relied on for support in the shelters. They were also denied interactions that suggested intimacy or a homelike comfort–things like bumming cigarettes or sharing clothing, sitting on other women's beds to talk were perceived as come-ons, and were often punished. Sexual minority women were required to wear more clothing in more areas of the shelter, and were subjected to a whole host of special, unwritten rules.

Sexual profiling was not limited to public institutions. Lela, a New Yorker from the Lower East Side, described her attempts to find respite from the shelters in a local hotel:

> It was 12:00 when we checked in. Alright. We get there and, and so Ann had the $30 out. And she goes, oh no, it's $50 for two women. So we just looked at her. We said $50? The thing is we thought the price was $30 a night. She said, well, no, well, my boss wrote this on the paper and she said for two men it's $50. For two women it's 50 and for a man and a woman it's $30 a night. There's a "couples only" that the $30 apply to.

CONCLUSION

Sexual minority women injectors are among the most vulnerable and least understood populations in terms of health risks and barriers to services (Committee on Lesbian Research Priorities, 1999). Increased HIV infection rates as well as higher levels of injection risks in this population do not seem to be related to the presence of gay or bisexual men in risk networks, nor to a sense that "lesbians don't get AIDS." Our study suggests that experiences of multiple marginalization are the most plausible explanation for sexual minority women injectors' increased HIV risks and infection relative to other drug injectors.

To understand the implications of this study, it is helpful to consider Kimberle Crenshaw's (1995) work on intersectionality, a term she uses in two senses. The first, structural intersectionality, describes how "multiple axes of subordination" shape the lived experiences of women of color. The second, political intersectionality, describes how feminist and antiracist *politics* and *discourse* regarding gender or racial subordination further marginalize women of color. Crenshaw's insights are readily transferred to the intersections that structure the lives of sexual minority women injectors, as well as to relevant arenas of HIV discourse that should–but fail to–address their situation.

Sexual minority women injectors are indeed "real" sexual minorities, although racism, classism, and prejudices against drug users block their recognition as such. This holds for both human interactions and discursive practices such as examination of "lesbians and AIDS" or "HIV among women drug users." As they are the women at highest risk in both groups, we must insist on making sexual minority women injectors the central concern of efforts to address HIV risk among both "lesbians" and women drug users.

REFERENCES

Clatts, M.C., Davis, W.R., & Atillasoy, A. (1995). Hitting a moving target: The use of ethnographic methods in the development of sampling strategies for the evaluation of AIDS outreach programs for homeless youth in New York City. *National Institute on Drug Abuse Research Monograph Series, 157*: 117-135.

Committee on Lesbian Research Priorities, Institute of Medicine (1999). *Lesbian health: Current assessment and directions for the future.* Washington, D.C.: National Academy Press.

Cooperman, N.A., Simoni, J.M., & Lockhart, D.W. (2003). Abuse, social support, and depression among HIV-positive heterosexual, bisexual, and lesbian women. *Journal of Lesbian Studies 7*, 49-66.

Crenshaw, K.W. (1995). Mapping the margins: Intersectionality, identity politics, and violence against women of color. In Crenshaw, K.W., (Ed.) *Critical race theory* pp. 357-383. New York: The New Press.

Friedman, S.R., Curtis, R., Neaigus, A., Jose, B., & Des Jarlais, D.C. (1999). *Social networks, drug injectors lives, and HIV/AIDS.* New York: Kluwer Academic/Plenum Publishers.

Friedman, S.R., Jose, B., Deren, S., Des Jarlais, D.C., & Neaigus, A. (1995). Consortium NAR. Risk factors for Human Immunodeficiency Virus seroconversion among out treatment drug injectors in high and low seroprevalence cities. *American Journal of Epidemiology, 142*, 864-874.

Hollibaugh, A.L. (June 1994). Transmission, transmission, where's the transmission? *Sojourner.*

Jose, B., Friedman, S.R., Curtis, R., Grund, J.P., Goldstein, M., Ward, T.P., &, Des Jarlais, D.C. (1993). Syringe-mediated drug-sharing (backloading): A new risk factor for HIV among injecting drug users. *AIDS, 7*, 1653-1660.

Kennedy, M.B., Scarlett, M.I., Duerr, A.C., & Chu, S.Y. (1995). Assessing HIV risk among women who have sex with women: Scientific and communication issues. *Journal of the American Medical Women's Association, 50*, 103-107.

Krieger, N. (2001). A glossary for social epidemiology. *Journal of Epidemiology and Community Health*; 55, 693-700.

Kwakwa H.A., & Ghobrial M.W. (2003). Female-to-female transmission of human immunodeficiency virus. Clinical Infectious Diseases 36(3): E40-E41.

Maher, L. (1997) *Sexed work: Gender, race and resistance in a Brooklyn drug market.* Oxford: Clarendon Press.

Neaigus, A.; Friedman, S.R.; Kottiri, B.J.; & Des Jarlais, D.C. (2001). HIV risk networks and HIV transmission among injecting drug users. *Evaluation and Program Planning 24*, 221-226.

Ompad, D.C., Maslow, C., C, Young, R.M. et al. (2003). HIV prevalence, social marginalization, risk behaviors, and high-risk sexual and injection networks among young women injectors who have sex with women. *American Journal of Public Health, 93*, 902-906, 2003.

Reyes, N. (January 9, 1991). Invisible science: Lesbians and AIDS. *Outweek*, 12-15.

Sterk, C.E. (1999). *Fast lives: Women who use crack cocaine.* Philadelphia: Temple University Press.

Young, R. (November, 2003). Sexualized surveillance of non gender-conforming women. American Anthropological Association Annual Meeting, Chicago, IL.

Young, R.M., Friedman, S.R., Case, P., Asencio, M.A., & Clatts, M. (2000). Women injection drug users who have sex with women exhibit increased HIV infection and risk behaviors. *Journal of Drug Issues, 30*, 499-524.

Young, R. (1994). The scarcity of data on cunnilingus. *The AIDS Reader, 4*, 132-133.

Young, R., Weissman, G., & Cohen, J. (1992). Assessing risk in the absence of information: HIV risk among women Injection drug users who have sex with women. *AIDS and Public Policy Journal, 7*, 175-183.

Index

Page numbers followed by the letter "t" designate tables.

Abuse, childhood sexual, 96
Acquired immune deficiency
 syndrome. See HIV/AIDS
 risk
Addiction treatment. See Recovery;
 Treatment
Adult Children of Alcoholics
 (ACOAs), 96
Affirmative Counselor Behavior Scale,
 83-84
Age
 abstention from alcohol and, 41-42
 alcohol-related social problems, 38-39,39t
 alcohol use/abuse and, 2-3,31-44
 demographics of cohort study, 36,37t
 depression and, 13
 drinking levels and, 36-37,38t
Alcoholics Anonymous (A.A.), 3-4, 74-75
 heterosexism and religiosity in, 96
 recovery and, 62
Alcohol use/abuse
 age and, 31-44,38t
 CHLEW Study, 31-44
 depression and, 2,7-18,14t. See also
  Depression
 disease model of, 3-4
 "maturing out," 3,41
 National Alcohol Survey (2000), 19-30
 patterns of, 22-23

 personal experience with, 69-78
 race/ethnicity and, 2-3,31-44,38t
 research paradigms, 91-101
 self-esteem and, 3
 social consequences of, 24-26,25t, 38-39,39t
 social identity and, 45-56
 social perceptions of, 72
 treatment issues, 73-74
Attitudes
 medical providers, 112-113
 social institutions, 113-114

Barnard College, 103-116
Bars. See Lesbian bars
Bisexuals
 HIV/AIDS risk and, 106-108
 marginalization of, 27

Center for Drug Use and HIV
 Research, 103-116
Childhood sexual abuse, 96
CHLEW Study
 background and principles, 32-33
 data analysis, 35-36
 demographics, 36,37t
 depression, 7-18,14t
 discussion, 40-42
 drinking levels, 36-37,38t
 instrument and measures, 34-35
 limitations, 42

methods, 33-36
participants, 33
race/ethnicity, 2-3,31-44
results, 36-40
Condom use, 109-110
(University of) Connecticut, 31-44
Counselors, sexual orientation of, 4
Critical Social research paradigm, 97-98

Depression
    alcohol use/abuse and, 2
    background and principles, 8-9
    conclusions, 16
    data analysis, 11
    demographics, 12t
    discussion, 13-16
    epidemiology, 8
    instrument, 9-10
    lesbians vs. general female population, 15
    limitations of study, 16
    measures, 10
    methods, 9-11
    predictors of, 14t
    results, 11-13,12t
    sampling and recruitment, 9
Drug use
    alcohol use/abuse and, 23-24
    injection-related risks, 108. *See also* HIV/AIDS risk

Empirical Post Positivist research paradigm, 92-95
Ethnicity. *See* Race/ethnicity
Ethnography, of HIV/AIDS risk, 103-116. *See also* HIV/AIDS risk

Families, recovery and, 63-64

Gay bars. *See* Lesbian bars
Gay identity model, 46-47

Geographic issues, in recovery, 65
Grounded theory, of recovery, 57-68. *See also* Recovery

Harvard University, 103-116
Heterosexism
    Alcoholics Anonymous and, 96
    medical providers, 112-113
HIV/AIDS risk, 103-116
    bisexuality and, 108-110
    condom use, 109-110
    demographics, 107
    drug use and injection-related risks, 108
    ethnographic study, 103-116
    information gap and, 110-111
    institutional attitudes and, 113-114
    lesbian invulnerability myth, 105-106,109-110
    lesbian networks and, 113
    marginalization and, 4
    medical provider attitudes and, 112-113
    methods, 106-108
    multiple marginalization and, 111-114
    preliminary hypotheses, 105-106
    "sex dam" use, 110
    sexual identity and relationships of sample, 107-108
    social support and, 111-112
    terminology of studies, 104-105
Homophobia. *See also* Self-acceptance
    internalized, 3
    of medical providers, 112-113
    religion and, 65-66

(University of) Illinois at Chicago, 7-18
Information, lack of and AIDS risk, 110-111
Injection-related risks, 108. *See also* HIV/AIDS risk

Index

Institutional attitudes, 113-114
Interpretive research paradigm, 95-97

Kentucky University, 45-56

Lesbian bars, 3,26
   social identity and, 53
   social networking and, 27
   as social structure, 71-72
Lesbian invulnerability myth, 105-106, 109-110
Lesbian networking, 3,105
   bars and, 27
   HIV/AIDS risk and, 106-108,113
   recovery and, 64
Lesbians
   categorization of, 2
   disaggregating combined populations, 2
   as invisible minority, 1
   marginalization of, 4,27,111-114
Lesbian style, 71-72

Marginalization, 4
   of bisexuals, 27
   HIV/AIDS risk and, 4,111-114

Narcotics Anonymous (N.A.), 62
National Alcohol Survey (2000), 2, 19-30
   background and principles, 20-21
   data analysis, 22
   discussion, 26-28
   limitations of study, 28
   measures, 22
   methods, 21-22
   results, 22-23
   social consequences, 24-26,25t
National Study of Health and Life Experiences in Women (HLEW) questionnaire, 9-10

Networking. *See* Lesbian networking
Non-Heterosexist Organizational Climate Scale, 84

Pennsylvania State University, 57-68, 79-90

Race/ethnicity
   abstention from alcohol and, 41-42
   alcohol-related social problems, 38-39,39t
   alcohol use/abuse and, 2-3,31-44
   demographics, 36,37t
   drinking levels, 36-37,38t
Recovery. *See also* Treatment
   background and principles, 58
   categories, 61-62
   central phenomenon, 61-62
   data analysis, 60-61
   discussion, 66-67
   families and, 63-64
   geographical issues, 65
   grounded theory and, 57-68
   learning recovery, 63
   method, 58-60
   participants, 60
   personal account of, 3-4,69-78
   relationships and, 63-64
   religion and spirituality and, 65-66
   results, 60-66
   self-acceptance and, 3,66-67
   self-identification and, 64-65
Religion/spirituality
   Alcoholics Anonymous and, 96
   homophobia and, 65-66
   recovery and, 65-66
Research paradigms, 4,91-101
   conclusions, 98
   Critical Social, 97-98
   Empirical Post Positivist, 92-95
   Interpretive, 95-97

San Jose State University, 19-30
Seattle University, 91-101

Self-acceptance, recovery and, 3,57-68, 66-67
Self-esteem
　alcohol use/abuse and, 3
　substance use and, 52t, 53
"Sex dam" use, 110
Sexual orientation
　blanket categorization by, 21
　categorization of, 28
　families and, 63-64
Social consequences, 24-26,25t, 38-39,39t
Social identity, 45-56
　aim of study, 47-48
　background and principles, 46-47
　conclusions, 54
　demographics, 51t
　design and procedure, 48-50
　discussion, 51-53
　gay identity model, 46-47
　limitations of study, 53-54
　methods, 47-50
　results, 50,51t, 52t
　substances used by participants, 52t
　substance use and, 45-56
　theoretical considerations, 46-47
Social identity theory, 46-47
Social research paradigms. *See* Research paradigms

Social support, HIV/AIDS risk and, 111-112
Substance use/abuse. *See* Alcohol use/abuse; Drug use

Tobacco use, alcohol use/abuse and, 21,23-24
Treatment, 79-90. *See also* Alcoholics Anonymous
　counselor orientation and, 4
　demographics, 82-83
　discussion, 86-88
　instruments, 83-84
　issues concerning, 73-74
　limitations of study, 88-89
　literature review, 80-82
　method, 82-85
　past and alcohol abuse, 27-28
　procedures, 85
　realities of, 75
　recommendations for, 75-76
　results, 85-86
Twelve-step programs, 62,74-75,96, 97-98

University of Connecticut, 31-44
University of Illinois at Chicago, 7-18

BOOK ORDER FORM!

Order a copy of this book with this form or online at:
http://www.haworthpress.com/store/product.asp?sku=5705

Making Lesbians Visible in the Substance Use Field

____ in softbound at $19.95 ISBN-13: 978-1-56023-617-7 / ISBN-10: 1-56023-617-5.
____ in hardbound at $39.95 ISBN-13: 978-1-56023-616-0 / ISBN-10: 1-56023-616-7.

COST OF BOOKS ____

POSTAGE & HANDLING ____
US: $4.00 for first book & $1.50
for each additional book
Outside US: $5.00 for first book
& $2.00 for each additional book.

SUBTOTAL ____
In Canada: add 7% GST. ____

STATE TAX ____
CA, IL, IN, MN, NJ, NY, OH, PA & SD residents
please add appropriate local sales tax.

FINAL TOTAL ____
If paying in Canadian funds, convert
using the current exchange rate,
UNESCO coupons welcome.

❑ **BILL ME LATER:**
Bill-me option is good on US/Canada/
Mexico orders only; not good to jobbers,
wholesalers, or subscription agencies.

❑ Signature ____

❑ Payment Enclosed: $ ____

❑ **PLEASE CHARGE TO MY CREDIT CARD:**
❑ Visa ❑ MasterCard ❑ AmEx ❑ Discover
❑ Diner's Club ❑ Eurocard ❑ JCB

Account # ____

Exp Date ____

Signature ____
(Prices in US dollars and subject to change without notice.)

PLEASE PRINT ALL INFORMATION OR ATTACH YOUR BUSINESS CARD

Name		
Address		
City	State/Province	Zip/Postal Code
Country		
Tel	Fax	
E-Mail		

May we use your e-mail address for confirmations and other types of information? ❑Yes ❑No We appreciate receiving your e-mail address. Haworth would like to e-mail special discount offers to you, as a preferred customer.
We will never share, rent, or exchange your e-mail address. We regard such actions as an invasion of your privacy.

Order from your **local bookstore** or directly from
The Haworth Press, Inc. 10 Alice Street, Binghamton, New York 13904-1580 • USA
Call our toll-free number (1-800-429-6784) / Outside US/Canada: (607) 722-5857
Fax: 1-800-895-0582 / Outside US/Canada: (607) 771-0012
E-mail your order to us: orders@haworthpress.com

For orders outside US and Canada, you may wish to order through your local
sales representative, distributor, or bookseller.
For information, see http://haworthpress.com/distributors

(Discounts are available for individual orders in US and Canada only, not booksellers/distributors.)

Please photocopy this form for your personal use.
www.HaworthPress.com

BOF05